SNOWMASS ANGEL

Danielle Coulter Biography

Check Out My Website

http://www.dancanshred.com

"For three years Danielle, has flooded my Facebook Timeline with Happiness and Joy. She is an Angel with CP"

Carla Wynn Hall

Snowmass Angel the Biography of Danielle Coulter

SNOWMASS ANGEL

Published by Soulful Pen Publishing

www.TheSoulfulPen.com

This is me with my new puppy Sage! My dog Jewells passed away in November, 2016 and she was 15 years old. Sage is my new puppy and I love her just as much.

Contents

A True Friend

By Carla Wynn Hall

I first met Danielle about 3-years ago, when on Facebook doing some work with her friend Win Kelly Charles. The first thing I noticed about Danielle was her contagious smile and the way it laminated the world. Danielle and I quickly became friends and have done several Skype calls and Google calls together just to have fun and chat.

Danielle is a 5-time author of the series about a young character named Zoe who loves to ski, but gets into trouble just like regular kids do. Danielle is a professional snowboarder and shreds the slopes at Challenge Aspen. Her motto is Dream It – Live It and she does this every day.

In the Spring Danielle and her clown friends bring more smiles to the children. Danielle also was Olaf also. The one thing I want to say is that Danielle was born with Cerebral Palsy. In her first book Dan Can Shred, she tells her story of how her life was as a child with CP. Her Zoe books are fun children's books that are written as fun novels. I have had the honor of being her editor and publisher, leaving her voice just as she writes. I am so proud of her.

Danielle was recently featured in The Aspen Times for her clowning part as DaniDoll!

Snowmass Angel the Biography of Danielle Coulter

Snowmass Angel the Biography of Danielle Coulter

A collection of short stories by Danielle P. Coulter a young entertainer, author and athlete who plays DaniDoll the Clown at Snowmass Village in Colorado. Danielle was born with Cerebral Palsy by has never let that stop her from changing the world.

The Biggest Transition in my Life

Moving to Snowmass

The biggest transitional time in my life was moving from Kansas City, Missouri to Snowmass Village, Colorado. When I was living in Kansas City, I was not as autonomous as I am living in Snowmass Village. When I had appointments, or wanted to see family, someone had to drive me. Kansas City doesn't have a great bus system like Snowmass does.

When I was growing up in Parkville I was loving my life. When I was in elementary school I woke up, went to school, and came back home to do my homework during the week. On the weekends, I used to go to play with my friends. Once I hit middle school everything changed for me. I got put in Special ED classes and only got to see my friends at school and not outside of school. I thought that they were moving through life and had forgotten about me. Throughout my school years and college, I thought everyday about being with my Challenge Aspen friends in Colorado. In December of 2013, my dream finally came true.

My first year living in Snowmass was a learning experience for me. My first winter I walked everywhere with my mom most of the time. She showed me how to walk on the ice and snow. I was scared but got the hang of it. Soon I was walking to the mall and to my snowboard lessons by myself. We live in a townhouse right at the base of Snowmass Mountain, so I can walk up to Base Village and the mall by myself whenever I want to to be out or meet up with friends. I feel freer now than I did in Kansas City. I feel that I want to be outside every day; in Kansas City I felt like I was trapped like Rapunzel.

My mom still had to drive me to my appointments when they were down the road or in Aspen. I didn't care about that, because I could have time to talk to my mom and tell her everything that I did that day. She was too scared for me to ride the buses. In the summer, my mom changed and started letting me learn the bus system. I was so happy and we talked to Max's dad, Todd, who is a bus driver. Todd told me how to get to the Snowmass Chapel and back home for my music therapy. I was happy that my mom let me ride the buses. I had to learn all of the bus routes for everywhere that I needed to go, like the gym, the bank, the chapel for music therapy and play camp. Also, I was going on the RAFTA bus to go to Aspen to get my hair cut.

My first summer on the buses was fun, but when you don't know all of the bus routes it's a huge adventure. On the day of Challenge Aspen's play I was going to Max's house to ride with him down valley where we were performing our play, The Little Mermaid. I got up early to get the 7:36 AM bus to the rodeo lot, where the gym is. I knew that Max's house was right up the hill from the gym. When I got to the Rodeo Lot, I walked back to the playground and started up the hill to Max's house.

When I got to the house Max's mom, Katie, asked, "Why are you breathing so hard?" I told her what I did and she told me that there was a bus that comes up to the street. That was a hard way to learn that there was a faster bus route, but good exercise for me before I put on my 10 pound Ursula costume for the play.

Once I got the hang of going out of the house on my own, I felt free as a bird. I am now more independent than I was in Kansas City. I don't have to wait on someone to take me somewhere, now I can go whenever I want. I used to think just as Rapunzel did, "When will my life begin?" Now, I say my life has begun!

Bridging Bionics

The Magic of Innovation and Technology

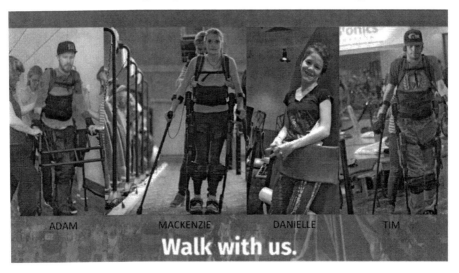

I am happy to be a part of **Bridging Bionics Foundation** at the Aspen Club in Aspen, Colorado. The foundation helps people who can't walk, walk again. First, a person gets on the Galileo Neuromuscular Tilt Table. The Galileo is a table that tilts to different degrees to help people to stand up on their feet. The feet are on a platform that vibrate your whole body. The tilt table helps reduces high tone so you can move better before you walk in the Ekso Skeleton. When you walk in the eLegs you get your body walking in perfect alinement. I wish I could walk in the Ekso Skeleton, but I am too short. I am happy that I can do the Galileo tilt table and the new Galileo smart dumbbell.

I do the dumbbell first, which helps my hands get looser. It looks like a box with a handle in the middle. I put my hands on the handle one at a time. The PT turns on the machine and the handle shakes up my hand to make it looser. When I am on the table the plate under my feet shake so the vibration goes up through my whole body. The frequency of the vibration can be lower and higher on the dumbbell and the table. They helped me a lot with my walking and my body can be looser. When I get finished with the two machines I walk around the gym with crutches. Since I am too short for the Ekso, I use the crutches to help me walk the right gait. After I workout, I feel really good.

Danielle Coulter

A Tribute to Bridging Bionics

www.BridgingBionicsFoundation.org

Bridging Bionics Foundation was created to bridge human mobility with bionic technology. One of the pillars of our mission is to help fund research and development projects that further the advancement of exoskeletons and bionic technologies so that we have more affordable and accessible global mobility solutions. While the field of bionic technology is relatively new, its application to human mobility issues presents barriers that may be solved through creativity and ingenuity.

Clowns and Magic

Do you believe?

I am Danielle Coulter with Cerebral Palsy. I work as a clown named Dannidoll the Rag Doll Clown. I love to make kids happy by doing bubbles and puppets around the Rocky Mountains Valley of Colorado.

Two years ago I ran into my friend, Tammy Bear, who owns Kid Toons Productions, a kid entertainment company. (I first met Tammy as Buttons at the first Magic of Music and Dance Camp.) My mom told her that we moved to Snowmass Village from Kansas City.

Tammy asked me if I wanted to work for her. I had to think about it for a while, because I had bad experiences in the past with clowns and magic, which I will get into later.

I thought how much I made kids happy for Variety Children's Charity of Greater Kansas City. Then I told myself to forget the past and look at the future. I can make kids happy by being a clown with Tammy. So, I called her up and told her that I wanted to be a clown.

Once I told Tammy that I wanted to be a clown, she asked me to meet her at Base Village in Snowmass Village, Colorado after a ski day where she and her team were working. So, I went up there to meet the team and started my clown training. I had a lot of fun with the team. Before I left for the day, Tammy told me that I walked like a rag doll and asked me to think about being a living rag doll. At first I thought how weird to be something that wasn't human. When I was young, my aunt, cousin, and I were watching a show about ventriloquists on TV. When they put a ventriloquist mask on a person, it weirded me out and I had to leave the room.

I thought about it and it was so cool that Tammy saw that I walked like a rag doll. I would have never known that. It would be cute to be a living rag doll clown. I put my faith into the character and became Dannidoll the Rag Doll Clown. Tammy and I put my costume together and learned that I could do puppets and bubbles. My hands are too shaky to do balloons or face paints.

I have a lot of fun playing with the kids and seeing their reactions. One boy asked to see how I move. I moved my arm from side to side like a rag doll. His mom told him that I don't have any bones in my body. I just laughed in my head. Funny stuff kids say.

Everyone knows Dannidoll is a fun little rag doll clown but in this book I will tell you my stories on my past with clowns and magic. This is my first time writing this for you. After you read this you may be asking the same thing that I asked myself, "How did I ever become a clown?"

Before I met Buttons the Clown, I remember that my dad was really into magic. One night my dad was watching a magic variety show on TV. He told me to come watch TV with him. So, I was about four or five and without knowing what was on, I crawled over to him. What I saw was people getting sawed in half and into thirds. I didn't like it at all and hide under the bed sheets. That was when I didn't want to see magic ever again.

Before I go on, I want to tell you that I had to remind my dad about the TV show. He didn't remember that he had done that to me. The next story I will be telling you, my dad had to remind me of.

When I was five years old, I met Buttons the Clown at the first Magic of Music and Dance Camp. The campers and I were in the gym at the Aspen Club. I was having a great time when Buttons was making balloons for everyone. Once Buttons said, "It's magic time!" I remembered what I saw on the TV and I hurried out of the gym like a bat out of hell.

I didn't want to be around magic. My dad was there and was worried that I ran out of the room. He didn't want me to fear magic.

As the years went by, Dad was trying to take me into our local pizza restaurant on magic night. I refused to go in as many times as I could. My dad didn't like it because he really wanted to show me that magic was not something to be afraid of. So, he went on he own.

One day I agreed to go. So, my dad took me into Stone Canyon Pizza. My dad introduced me to Gene the magician. He told Gene that he didn't want me to be scared of magic anymore. Gene showed me slight of hand magic with balls and coins, which I really love. Then I was into it. My dad and Gene gave me a lot of magic kits with magic tricks that I could do with my hands. I would have never known that magic was so cool if I had seen the right magic tricks first.

As the years past I felt more comfortable going into restaurants with my dad at magic nights in Kansas City and Snowmass Village. Plus, being around Buttons the Clown helped, too. Soon, I was doing magic shows in my school's talent shows with my friends and sometimes by myself. It was amazing.

I still am afraid of the magic that I saw on TV and can't be around it. Like once, I was watching Reading Rainbow and before Lamar Burton got sawed into half, I ran out of the bedroom and into the bathroom. Can't even watch movies or TV shows if I know there is magic tricks like that in the show. I just turn it off.

It was so bad that in my senior year of high school, I was in my Language Art class on the first day back from Spring Break. We were watching a documentary about a magician- Houdini. It was his birthday. I was watching it as much as I could. When the video was talking about sword swallowing, I couldn't watch anymore. I went back to working on my assignment. (The next part on what happened was due to what was on the video and partly due to my cold. I got a cold before my spring break week, and I snowboard all week long with a cold because I only got to do what I love to do one week out of the year. I didn't want to miss it.)

As I was working on my assignment, my stomach was starting to hurt. So, I laid my head down on my desk. Soon, I woke up with everyone around me. I started to cry, I didn't realize that I had blanked out. My teachers and classmates was worried about me. They thought that I had a seizure. They got me into a wheelchair and wheeled me to the nurse's office. I was crying so much that they couldn't understand me. The nurse called my mom to tell her what happened. Soon, the nurse handed me the phone. I told my mom what really happened. When I talked to her, it made me feel better. After the call, I felt better, put myself back together, and went back to class. My mom thinks that I had a bad past life where I got hurt with something sharp, and I think that is true.

Now, I told you about magic and it is time to talk about clowns. When I was eight or nine years old, my dad took my friends and me to the Ringling Brothers and Barnum & Bailey Circus. All day long my friends and I were excited to go. We were jumping on the trampoline all afternoon before it was time to go. It was my first circus and I couldn't wait to see all of the acts. During the show, I loved the animals, high flying and daring acts, but there was one big clown act that I didn't like at all.

A lady clown walked into a pizza shop to order a pizza. While she was waiting, the cooks were making the pizza. As one of the cooks was rolling out the pizza dough, another cook's hand got caught between the dough and the rolling pin. He got rolled right into the pizza dough! When I saw that, I covered my eyes with my hands. I begged my dad to take me out of there, but he wanted to stay. I tried to peak out between my fingers and watch, but I couldn't. All I remember was the pizza going into the oven and the cook that fell into the dough popping out of the chimney all bunt up. That act scared me so bad that I couldn't wait to get out of there.

When it comes down to clowns, I only like what Buttons the clown does like face paint, balloon animals, and kid magic. I don't know why circus clowns scared me but Buttons made me happy. That's why I said yes to be a clown. I decided to forget about the past to make kids happy and be with my friends who I met when I was just five years old. I had put all of my faith into Tammy and Dannidoll.

During my first summer of being Dannidoll, I was working every Sunday at the Family Fun Day at Base Village. When I wasn't working, people were telling me that an Italian family circus named, Zoppe, was coming to town at the end of summer. Everyone who told me was excited about it because a circus had never come into Snowmass Village before. When people talked about the circus, I acted like I was excited also. I really wasn't happy to hear about it because of the clown act that I saw when I was a kid. I didn't want to go. As the time got closer, my mom was talking about it daily. She asked me if I wanted to go and I said no. She told me that the circus will be different because it was small and only had dogs and a pony animal acts. I ignored her, and soon she bought tickets for her, myself, and my stepdad. I told myself okay, now I have to go.

Snowmass Angel the Biography of Danielle Coulter

Every day before the circus opened I saw the big tent during the day and night time. It really creeped me out at night time. I was hoping that I would be okay on show day. Soon Saturday came and we went to the show and we watched the pre-show outside of the tent. We were in the back so I could barely see. It sounded really fun, but I was nervous. I hoped that there were no big magic tricks.

When the pre-show ended, everybody started going inside the tent. When we got inside I looked around. I loved the inside of the tent. There was popcorn, a little hot air balloon by the trapeze, and fun music playing. I was feeling better, but my stomach still hurt with nerves. One of the ushers tried to help us find seats for us. My mom bought the cheap tickets and we were getting the seats on the bleachers in the back. I set on the first row, because it is hard for me to climb up. The usher saw that I didn't have a good view. She asked if we would like to move up to the first row, and we said yes. Somehow the people who bought the first-row seats didn't show up. It was cool that I could see everything, but I still was nervous.

When the show began, everyone came out to welcome us to the show with dancing and balls bouncing around. I was starting to feel better. As the show went on I saw a dog act, high flying acts, and clowns acts with Nino and his brother with no magic what-so-ever. I loved it. Before I knew it, it was intermission. I finally relaxed. I knew that I was having fun and didn't have to be scared anymore.

During intermission, I went to buy a Nino doll so I could have a clown doll when I was working as Dannidoll. Once I sat down, I put the doll in my lap. Five minutes' letter, Nino was walking by and saw the doll in my lap. He went to get his other doll and gave it to me. I was surprised and I thanked Nino. My mom told me to tell Nino that I would be a clown tomorrow. Once Nino came around again, we told him. Nino said, "Cool, I'll come by and see you tomorrow!" When I heard that it made me more excited.

Once the second haft of the show began, I was having the time of my life. I would have never known that I would have fun at a circus or make a friend with a circus clown. After the show, everybody who was in the show went outside. When I got out of the tent, I saw Nino and thanked him for the doll. He said welcome and pulled me to a table to give me a book and a t-shirt. The rest of the night I was in shock about the day's events.

The next day, Nino saw me saw me as a clown and gave me a hug. He told me that he really liked my costume. I told my friend Penny, who I was working with, what happened the day before at the Zoppe Circus.

After I told Penny the story, she wanted to take a picture with him. When we were done working we saw Nino outside of the tent. We took a quick picture with him, because he had to go into the tent once the music was over. I was happy that the timing worked out, and took a picture with him as Dannidoll.

Once I got home, I changed out of my costume. My mom told me that I should give Nino one of my books. I got a copy of my bio and hurried back up to Base Village. I saw Nino outside for intermission and gave him the book. He was happy and said thanks. Nino asked me if I wanted to see the second half of the show, and I said yes. He pulled me into the tent to see the show. I was on cloud nine! After the show, I took a picture as myself with me in Nino's arms. It was an amazing weekend.

On Monday, I ran into Nino again and we said hi. I gave him my card and he asked if I wanted to do an act with him next year; maybe the trapeze? I was too embarrassed at the time and all that I could do was shake my head no. He told me that I hope to see you next year. Later that day I found him on Facebook and sent him a message about doing an act. So, we will see what will happened this year, in 2016.

Now that I told you my life story with clowns and magic, you might think that I am crazy. Sometimes, I think why did I ever say yes to be a clown, but I am happy that I did. Every time that I work with Tammy and her team, I have a great time making the kids happy. When you are a clown you'll never know, what will happen, like running in the rain with Buttons the Clown singing "Singing in the Rain" on the top of your lungs.

My Friend Max

Frozen Sing a Long

I met Max at the first Magic of Music and Dance Camp at the Aspen Club 20 years ago. Max has CP also, but can't walk or speak. We became great friends over the years of acting in the camp. One year the play was Annie. I was Annie and Max was Sandy. I was happy to sing Tomorrow right next to him. I was so happy to make him happy by my singing. Once I moved out to Snowmass we get together to go to yoga, bowling, see movies, and sing together in a singing group called Aspen Noise. Being around him more I learned how he communicates with his hand and face. It always makes me feel happy when I make him smile.

For Christmas Eve I was Olaf the snowman at Base Village in Snowmass Village. It was the first day of Family Fun at Après on the Bricks. Family Fun at Après on the Bricks is a weekly event that is a part of the Very Important Kid program in Snowmass. The program puts on fun activities every day after kids ski. In November, my friend, Tammy, told me that I would be with Elsa and Anna on Christmas Eve. She told me that we need to figure out who I will be. That same night I went online to look at Olaf costumes.

I looked at the costumes by Disney and they were all jumpsuits. I can't wear a jumpsuit because I can't go to the restroom on my own due to my CP. I found an Olaf tutu on Esty that was homemade. On the white tutu there are 3 black balls for the snowman buttons and for the top was Olaf's face. I thought it was so cute. I also found an Olaf coat that looks like a snowman body and has Olaf's face on the hoodie on eBay. I told Tammy what I found and she loved the idea. So my mom helped me find the right size. I found the right size for the coat and I had to email the maker who makes the tutu to see how her size chart works. One I found the right size I ordered it on Black Friday. The website said to check on it on shipping day witch is on December 16th. On that day I checked on it and it hadn't shipped. With the little energy that I had of being sick, I emailed her to tell her that I was a part of a kid entertainment group and what I was doing on Christmas Eve. She told me that she didn't have the cotton top yet but she could give me the t-shirt and have it mailed out by Monday. I said yes and thanked her. The next morning I got an email from her that she had mailed it out that morning. Even though I had to cancel my day activities because I was stick, I was happy that my Olaf tutu was on it's way. It came two days before Christmas Eve. I was so grateful that it came in the nick of time. I didn't want to let down my team and didn't have any idea of what to be if the tutu didn't come. On Christmas Eve every kid came up to me and said hi. I had a blast being Olaf.

My Ireland Trip

The Elders and Good Times

In October 2016, I went to Ireland on my uncle's band, The Elders, tour for my 3rd time in my life. Every year The Elders who are an Irish rock band take their fans on a tour of Ireland. It's a lot of fun.

We are in Ireland for ten days and every other day we move to a different town. It is hard to move every other day when you have CP, but it is worth it to get to see every thing and hear my uncle play in the band.

Every time I have been to Ireland, it's always a new adventure for me. I have been in castles, pubs, and old houses. I even have been where they make Irish whiskey and Guinness. In 2014, we went to see how the Irish whiskey was made. After the tour we did a testing. You'd think that I was going to pass on it because of my CP. Well, it was my holiday and I joined in with everybody else. I did my testing with my straw. I can't drink anything without a straw. After we were finished, I told my mom that I was a little dizzy. She had to help me back on the bus. When you are as little as me, a little alcohol can mess you up big time.

In the three years that I was in Ireland, my favorite place that I have visited is the Aran Island. We took a 45 minute ferry ride to get there. When we got on the Island, we took a little tour of it. It was a beautiful little island with cute little houses and horse carriages. After about 30 minutes we stopped somewhere. I had no idea what we were about to do. We walked to a little courtyard and our tour guide handed us tickets. I took my Mom's arm and started walking up a pathway up a hill. We were walking on gravel and my right foot was turning in a lot. A man who was on the tour with us asked if we needed help. I told him yes and my Mom asked me why? I told her about my right foot.

As we were walking we could see the green grass and a lot of beautiful plants. We also saw old rocks that were for a fort for some time in the past. The Wild Atlantic Ocean was in our view the whole way up the hill. The sound of the waves hitting the cliffs was powerful and beautiful to hear. One of my friends past us and told me, "I thought that I wouldn't see you here, but here you are." I told her yep and I thought this was going to be a long way up before we get to wherever we were going.

After a while, the gravel path turned into a rocky hill that lead up to a fort. As we started up the rocky hill, we wound our way up and picked out the easiest way up. People were calling me a mountain goat when they saw me going up. We finally arrived at an archway that led into the fort, the view gave me a breath of fresh air. The view was amazing. The grass was an Irish green and some rock form the fort was in the ground. You can see the waves coming up on the cliffs, because one of the walls of the ring fort had fallen off at some point in time. My mom and I heard my aunt yelling at us that we made it and to come up to the second level of the fort. So we went on up.

When we got up to the second level, we looked over the wall and at some point I sat right by the edge and looked out at the view. It was amazing and I took in everything that I saw. It felt like I was in a dream, but it was real. It was worth all of my energy to climb that huge hill to see an amazing view from the ring fort. When I got back down to the little courtyard, I had to put my arms out like airplane wings to keep my balance to get over to the picnic table to set down. I was tired and my legs were like noodles. I was so tired but it was worth it. It was a story to tell and I am happy that I just told it to you.

It is a lot of fun when your uncle is in an Irish rock band and you can go on tour with him in Ireland. It's always fun to see old friends, family, and make new friends. Also you can jig the whole night away when the band is playing in a pub. Every time I go to Ireland it is always a party and a new adventure.

Chapter Three – Playing the Xylophone

Improving my Arm Movements

A lot of people have seen me play the xylophone for the past two years in shows, but I want to tell you that there is a lot more feeling behind my playing than making myself and other people happy. In early 2015, my music therapy teacher, Mack Bailey, brought in a little xylophone called a glockenspiel. Mack wanted to see if it would help me with my arm movements.

At first my arms were out of control. They went way up over my head every time I hit a note. Also, I was hitting more notes than one. I did drills and worked on it hard and my hands got better and I was playing songs. I told Mack that I really loved to play the xylophone. I also told him that I had a great grandfather who I had never met who played the xylophone.

My great grandfather, Charlie Pryor, played the xylophone awesomely well. I heard stories and saw videos of him playing music. My favorite story of him was that he could play the Flight of the Bumblebee with two mallets in each hand as fast as he could. My aunt showed me that video and it was amazing. Now that I play the xylophone, I wish I had met Charlie, but I am happy to carry on the tradition of his xylophone playing.

When spring came up, Mack (also the director of the Magic of Music and Dance Camp) told me that he wanted to do a play that would tell the campers' stories with John Denver's songs. Mack asked me if I wanted to sing and play Sunshine on my Shoulders on the xylophone. He also asked me if I could be Dannidoll the Rag Doll Clown because the song fit her. I was excited and said yes! As the time went by I was getting better at playing the xylophone and the word got out about what I was doing. People were asking me to play at events before I did my performance in the play.

My snowboarding teacher, Rich, asked me to play at the Deaf Camp Picnic. Challenge Aspen wanted me to play and sing Sunshine on my Shoulders as Dannidoll at the Amy Grant and Vince Grill Gala. How could I say no? With the three events within a week and two days of working as a clown, I would make time to do it. That is what performers do, right? Take as many gigs as they can without overlapping? Right!

The Death Camp Picnic where people raise money to help the death people they put a music event together where bands play their music all day long. Every year my friends put together a John Denver tribute and sing his songs. Rich always asked me to sing a song with him in his music set and I said yes. When he heard that I was working on playing Sunshine on my Shoulders on the xylophone he asked me if I wanted to play and sing the song with him. I said yes. As the time got closer to the event, Rich was telling me that the song was so slow and long. He want to make our singing time more upbeat and fun. We decided to do a John Denver medley with Sunshine on my Shoulders, Country Road, and Grandmother's Feather Bed.

The plan was that I play the xylophone with "Sunshine on my Shoulders", then sing it with Rich, and then sing Country Road. When we got to Grandmother's Feather Bed we go crazy. When Rich sings about the food and stuff in the bed, I pull out the things out of a black bag and show them to the audience. At the end of the song both of us fell down on an air mattress with Feathers on it and go crazy. It was a lot of fun and everyone loved it.

For the play I had my friend, Max, act like he was sad and his helper held up a big rain cloud over his head. I came out as Dannidoll with three of my friends who were dressed up as clowns, also. I asked Max why he was sad. He told me that it was raining outside. My clown friends and I told the audience what made us happy. Then we went into Sunshine on my Shoulders. As I was playing the xylophone and singing the first part of the song, my friends stood in font of Max to hide him. Max was turning into a clown himself. When he came out again as a clown, he had a big sun over his head and was happy. Everyone joined in singing. It was a fun act to do when you get to turn your friend's frown upside down.

The following Monday after the play was the Amy Grant and Vince Gill Gala. Mack, Max, and I were asked to go and do our act as we did in the play by Challenge Aspen. We were happy to do it. We had to be there early before the event for our sound check. So, I packed up my party dress in my backpack and turned myself into Dannidoll with a little help from my mom. When I was all ready to go, I put on my backpack and took the bus to Max's house. It was fun to ride the bus as Dannidoll because when the bus driver saw me he told me that I looked colorful. That made me so happy that I felt that the night would go great. When Max and I got to the St. Regent Hotel where the event was and we met Mack. Before we did our sound check, all three of us had our photo taken with Max and I in our clown costumes. Max and I did the first two pictures together and then Mack stepped in for the last two. We had a blast in the photo area!

After we did a quick sound check we stayed in the backstage area until we went on. For the first time in five years that I had performed at this event it was freezing cold in the room. I never felt so cold in the ball room before. I only had my Dannidoll costume on with my rainbow tights on. I had to roll up in a ball on the floor to stay warm. Now I wish I had my black tights with me so I could put them on with my dress after the performance. I only had a shawl in my backpack and I put it on over my costume. It was orange and I was happy it went well with my costume.

An hour went by and the show started. I was so happy because we were about to go on to do our shorter version of our act because we didn't have everyone from the play. I was happy to do it but I couldn't wait to get out of the frozen ball room. When we heard our names we went on the stage. It was a little harder because we didn't have a lot of room to move. After we did our lines, I had to step over cords and slide by Mack to get to the xylophone. As I played the xylophone and sang the song with Mack and Max I was getting into it. After we finished everyone stood up and clapped. They loved it! When we got out of the ball room, somebody from Challenge Aspen told us that was the best you had ever done. When I heard that, it made me so happy.

Once I said my goodbyes to Max I ran to the bathroom to change. When I got into the bathroom I felt better, because it was the warmest room of the night. As I was changing, people were telling me how much they loved the act. It always takes me a while to get into and out of my Dannidoll character. I kinda make a joke to myself when I am getting out of Dannidoll. "I'm human again!" I came up with it based off of the song "Human Again" from the Broadway show Beauty and the Beast. I came up with it because Dannidoll is a rag doll clown. (I always wanted to be in Beauty and the Beast the moment that I saw the Broadway play as a kid in Kansas City. It's still one of my dreams to act in the play.)

Once I changed, I went back into the ball room to eat. The rest of the night was just fun relaxing and hearing music. It was fun because people was asking me "Were you the one who was on stage?" I said yes. Every time I heard that it made me laugh in my head. When you have a costume on and people don't realize that it is you, you have an awesome costume.

In the summer of 2016, the play camp did another play with the kids' stories but this time they told their dreams. Mack wanted me to talk about being an author and he told me that some campers love to write too. He wanted me to sing Bibbidi-Bobbide-Boo in the play, because writing a book is like magic. I loved the idea and was all in. I had been singing the song for months to help with relaxing every part of my mouth. I even told Mack that if we ever put on Cinderella I wanted to sing Bibbidi-Bobbide-Boo. My dream was coming true even though the play wasn't Cinderella. I had been working hard to sing the song and play it on the xylophone. Even though I don't talk as well as I want to, I sing with magic inside of me so people can understand every word that I sing. I don't know how this works, but I love it.

Mack also told me that I could be Dannidoll again if I wanted to. I had to think about it. Dannidoll was a part of my life, too. Later, I told my mom about what I was doing for the play and what Mack said about being Dannidoll again. She gave me an idea of being a fairy for the play because it goes well with the song and I love fairies. I had two great ideas that were dancing in my head. I loved them both and I was Dannidoll in the play the year before. I wanted to do something new. I thought to put the two ideas together and be Dannidoll the Fairy. I ran it by Mack before I bought my fairy stuff for Dannidoll. He loved it and that made me happy.

I bought purple fairy wings with a matching wand. I also found a red wig that was up in a bud just like a fairy has her hair up. I was so excited to sing and play the xylophone as Dannidoll the Fairy. Once again, I had fun playing the xylophone and singing with my friends for everyone in the audience.

Later in the fall, Mack wanted me to start learning how to read music while playing the xylophone. So, I brought in my Disney music books and started playing and reading songs on the xylophone. I had a lot of fun hearing the songs as I was playing the xylophone. It made me so happy when I could hear the songs as I played them. One day, Mack told me that now that I could read music, I could play with Aspen Noise. Aspen Noise is a singing group that I sing with at the Aspen Chapel. That same day I texted my friend, Barbara, who is the director of Aspen Noise. When I told her what Mack said, she got excited and said yes to having me play the xylophone with Aspen Noise.

A few weeks later, Barbara asked me if I would like to play the xylophone at the Thanksgiving service with a song called I'm Calling You. I said yes. The song is about being on a mountain calling your friends from another mountain. I told Mack and he showed me how to play the song on the xylophone. We didn't have a lot of time to practice, so he marked the xylophone with colored stick on dots, like my first year of playing it. I nailed it down as fast as I could and was ready to perform on Sunday, November 13th.

I was so excited to get a chance to play my music outside of Challenge Aspen, and have more people hear my music. On the Sunday after the service, people were coming up to me and thanking me for sharing my magic. It made me so happy to hear everyone telling me how much they loved my xylophone playing. Also, Barbara asked me if I wanted to play Feliz Navidad on the xylophone for the Sardy House Tree Lighting event in Aspen. When I heard that I was excited and told her that I was in!

For the two years that I was playing the xylophone in music therapy, I was happy to play in shows for Challenge Aspen for both my friends and family. And now, for everyone in the community with Aspen Noise. I am surprised that I had to work so hard on my hands and arms to play music for everyone. I am happy to make people happy by playing the xylophone. I know that Charlie Pryor's genes have been passed down to me because I love playing the xylophone for everyone. I wished that I had met him, but I know he is proud of me and watching every performance I do from heaven.

Snowmass Angel the Biography of Danielle Coulter

Physical Training

Keeping my Body in Shape to Do What I Love

As a snowboarder and an actor with CP who lives in Snowmass Village, I work out every day. Every morning I go to the Snowmass Rec Center to do the elliptical and once a week yoga. I want to keep my body strong and heathy so I can keep doing what I love to do.

Every morning I go to the Snowmass Rec Center to do the elliptical for 45 minutes a day. I want to keep my legs strong so I can keep walking and snowboarding. My step-dad told me if I don't work out every day I can go back in my walker or worse, a wheelchair. That is why I keep moving.

In the summer, I go to the Rec Center about every morning to do the elliptical and on Wednesday afternoons I do yoga to stretch out my body. When I have to work out on the Galileo or work as a clown in the mornings I skip the Rec Center. It seems that summer is easy for me, and you are right, but in winter it's another story.

In winter time, I work as a clown at the bottom of Snowmass Mountain after a ski day once a week. On that day, I wake up, get ready, eat, and go down to the Rec Center to get my workout in. After I work out, I go up to the mall to get something to eat and relax with the free time that I have. When it is time to get into my costume, I get on the little gondola that takes me to the bottom of Snowmass Mountain and walk as fast as I can back home.

Now you think that I get my workout only at the gym, no I don't. With little time on the line I have to walk as fast as I can. I don't care if I am running out of time, I want to work out as much as I can. I work out so I can walk, snowboard, and act as long as I can.

Losing Jewells

I was so sad to lose her.

Jewells was an amazing Border Collie. She was a one quarter Blue Heeler, also. As a puppy, she was given to my mom by her friend ferries-Dennis Tull. When she came to the house she and our other dog, Tag, followed me everywhere I crawled in the house. They loved me and I loved them.

Every day when I got home from school, Jewells was so happy to see me that she jumped up on me and pinned me to the floor and kissed me to death. She missed me so much when I was in school. When I was upset about something or hurt myself, she was right by my side kissing me or licking my boo boo. Jewells always knew when I needed someone to love on when I was feeling down.

As we both got older, Jewells loved to be in the car with my mom and me. Jewells always barked and kissed me a thousand times a minute. She always loved me and would go up to people to say hi. I always knew when my mom was coming to pick me up at school by Jewells's barking. Jewells went everywhere with us.

When we moved to Snowmass Village, Jewells walked up to the mall with us to Starbucks and would get a cup of whipped cream and eat food Crum's off of the floor. She also tried to say hi to everyone she met. She was so friendly that we thought that she would make a great Walmart greeter. Jewels also loved to go to Aspen Noise to see everyone and hear us sing.

In the fall of 2016, Jewels was slowing down in her walking. My mom and I were worried about her. My mom had to carry her when she didn't have the energy to walk anymore. She looked and acted like a puppy at age 15. Jewells loved us so much that she wanted to be with us as much as she could.

Jewells passed away in our own home in the early morning of Sunday, November 13th. I felt in my heart that she wanted to pass in the house instead of letting us put her down. Jewells wanted to do this, because she loved us so much and I know she is looking out for me every day.

My mom and I still act like Jewells is with us in the house and the car. It is not the same but I know that she is looking down on us every day. Jewells will always be in our hearts. I always will love her to the moon and back.

Falling in Love

The Joys of 6th Grade and Beyond

As I was growing up in Parkville, I thought it was hard to find a guy to fall in love with when you have CP. In 6th grade, when I thought everyone forgot about me, this guy whom I met in kindergarten made his move on me. It was totally unexpected.

That same year, my school put on an after-school party four times a year for the kids who have good grades. They have games, movies, food, and crafts. It's was called Paws because our mascot was the tiger. I was excited to go to the party because I knew I had good grades. For the first Paws I went with my friends from my Special ED class. We were having a blast, but once we got into the movie room to watch Scooby-Doo I felt something change in my body. The guy who I met in kindergarten was hanging out with me for the party. He waved me to the back of the room. I followed him but I didn't know what was going on.

Once I got back there he told me that he had been watching me throughout the school years and had been helping me without my knowledge. He loved my smile and attitude. He asked me to be his girlfriend. When I heard that, I was shocked, and it took me a moment to say yes! I said yes because he was funny and fun to be around. He always treated me well and I couldn't wait to learn more about him.

Once he asked me to be he girlfriend, we started hanging out outside of school a lot. I learned that he was totally a redneck. He loved Nascar, country music, Dukes of Hazard, and his favorite football team was the Green Bay Packers. He didn't like to perform in any way like me or watch Disney movies, except he introduced me to the Santa Clause movies and I loved them. We tried to push each other to like what the other person liked but it didn't work. We knew we loved each other and would go out to the movies, out to eat, and go to our favorite park - Worlds of Fun.

Worlds of Fun is a huge amusement park right outside of Kansas City. We went a lot with his family and his best friend. He called his best friend, Ron Weasley, because he has red hair and his whole family did, too. Yes, I know Harry Potter fans, and I am one, too. (My boyfriend had a Harry Potter costume and I had a Hermione costume. I wanted to go out together for Halloween as them, but it didn't happen.) Every time we went to the park my boyfriend pushed me around in a wheelchair and didn't want me to go on big rides. He always worried about me and wanted to protect me. When I wanted to go on a big rollercoaster, I had to ride with Ron because my boyfriend was to chicken to go. I don't know how many times I clucked and flapped my chicken wings at him. It was fun to tease him, too.

One day he surprised me by going with me on my favorite rollercoaster, the Patriot. It is the biggest and fastest loopt- a- loopt, feet dangling ride. I couldn't believe it! He helped me into my seat because I was too short to get over the bar that good between your legs. Once we were all set we took off. We were having fun but I was the only one who was yelling. After we were off we went to look for and buy our picture. In the picture I had my mouth wide open and he had a big smile on his face. When I look at that picture I don't know who is thinking what.

Our favorite time to go to Worlds of Fun was in October. In the daytime, it looked and felt like a Halloween town and at night haunted houses appeared. We went to some and it was lame but fun. We wanted to go to the good ones but the lines were too long. He and I love Halloween and tried to scare each other. Once I was at his house, talking to his mom in the living room. My boyfriend wasn't with me. I thought he was getting a Mountain Dew from his stash. He was gone for a long time and I wasn't thinking that something was up. Soon enough, I saw there was a guy standing outside the window with a white hockey mask on. It scared me half to death and soon realized that it was my boyfriend. When he came into the house, I hit him and tickled him! We were laughing so hard and soon realized that his mom was in on the plan to scare me, too. I was so mad at both of them. We had fun messing around with each other. But we stopped when it got overboard, like when non-eating stuff got in my mouth or getting a black eye on Valentine's Day. We stopped before it got too far.

Oh, I have to tell you one more thing that he did to me that was not funny to me then. But now it is funny, because I am a rag doll clown for crying out loud. We and a friend who was on a bus for a field trip and I was stuck in the middle of them. I don't know how this came up, but my boyfriend put his hand on my jaw and started moving my jaw up and down and talking in a high voice. I became his own puppet. My friend started laughing and joined in the fun. They started moving my arms also, like I wasn't human anymore. After a while I started to get annoyed by them and started to slap them silly. I didn't like it but after that day he started to call me his little puppet, which was cute.

Remember when I told you that my boyfriend made me do what he loves to do? When I tried to get him to do what I loved to do, I always lost. It made me sad when I always lost, but be careful what you wish for because you don't know who would jump in to help you when you don't ask for it. When we were in 8th grade, I was trying out for the school play and he was in choir for the second year in a row. All of our Special ED teachers and the choir teacher wanted my boyfriend in the choir. He was complaining about being in the class about everyday of the school year. He didn't like to sing, read music, or preform. He was driving me nuts.

Soon after I got a part in the school play, Aladdin, my boyfriend told me that the choir teacher/director of the play wanted him to be on stage crew for extra credit. My boyfriend didn't want to do it but he had no choice. Before he started working with the whole crew, he told me to keep our relationship a secret and don't tell the teacher. I agreed. By the way, everyday I was teasing him about being on the crew. It was really fun. But one day at rehearsal I fell down when I was not in my walker. (When I was in school from K-12th my teachers and physical therapists still wanted me to use my walker even though I could walk on my own. They didn't want me to fall and get hurt.) Everyone saw that I fell and the director wanted me to use my walker. That made me so mad because I could walk and fell a lot but I didn't want my freedom to be taken away from me. So the director and I somehow made amens. I could walk with a cane and my boyfriend had to be my right hand man backstage. I didn't like it but you have to do what a teacher tells you to do.

During all four shows my boyfriend was by my side the whole time except when he had to move sets in and out. When he was doing that he wanted me to sit down in a chair to rest when I wasn't out dancing and singing on stage. I didn't like it because I wanted to move around on my own like the way I did in the last play-Honk. I had to run around like crazy because I had to change costumes three times in the show. I like that instead of having to sit down and my boyfriend watching out for me every minute of the whole play. Plus, he was my behind the scene right hand man. He helped me move my walker in and out of tight places, helped me put my Friend Like Me costume over my town person costume, and handed me my magic trick from behind the curtain. I started to like having my boyfriend help me and bossing him around. But on the last night of the play something went wrong and we had to come up with a new plan.

Every night during Friend Like Me some of the kids showed off their talent and one of them was me. I had a yellow scarf that turned into a cane. The plan was when everyone else was playing their air trombones, I slid off stage and my boyfriend put my magic trick in my hand. We didn't have a lot of time to do the hand off. When everyone jumped back, I slipped in and did my trick and then handed off the cane to my boyfriend and went back to my place. It felt like an old play routine with stuff going in and out.

On the last night of the play when I came off the stage for One Jump Ahead to get ready for Friend Like Me, my boyfriend came up to me when I was changing. He said, "I don't know how this happened but it wasn't me." He then showed me my slinky up cane that popped out on him. I didn't believe him and started to blame him but after awhile I believed he didn't do it. With panic rising inside of me, I took the broken cane and wrapped it up so it was a cane again. I asked somebody to go get our director to set up the trick again but he was in the light and sound area and not backstage with us. I was in a panic and didn't know what to do when it was time to do my trick. My friend told me that she would get into the Genie's magic bag and get me a handful of sparkle dust. When she put it in my hand I said thanks.

I was running a little late because of the trick delay and I told my boyfriend to hurry up with my walker. Every night he had to roll my walker though a tight tunnel so I didn't move the stage curtains so everyone couldn't see out movement. As I was running I was thinking of how in the heck would I make it through this scene with only one hand free to drive my walker. I was scared out of my mind. Guess all actors have a mess up once or twice, but when you have CP it is another level of stress. I didn't know if I could dance with one hand driving my walker. Here I go, ready or not! Before I heard my cue, I looked back and didn't see my boyfriend or my walker. Oh no, what was I going to do?

When I heard my cue, I jumped out in line without thinking, and I did my first dance move without my walker or falling down. The next dance move was a move that I couldn't do fast enough and move aside like all of the nights before. I was happy to see my walker rolling right to me. My boyfriend made it and pushed out my walker in time. I grabbed it with my free hand. My other hand had the sparkles in it so I only put my wrist on the other handle. Now I felt better but with only one hand and a wrist on my walker, I couldn't wait to let my sparkles fly.

Once we got to the air trombone part, I stayed in line and played my air trombone for the first time with everyone else, so it would look normal for the audience. When everyone jumped back, I went forward and did a little dance and let my sparkles fly. I could hear my director laughing so loud, because he didn't know what was going on. When you are an actor anything can happen that you can't fix so you have to improvise. So it is fun when you can boss your boyfriend around. He did a great job for his first and last play that he would work on with me.

When we got into high school, I had to go in a school in Kansas, because my mom was living with her boyfriend and who is now my stepdad. It was hard for my boyfriend and me to live in two different states and go to different schools. But every weekend one of us would cross the state border to see each other. Plus, we would try to go to each other's dances. It was fun because we went to two Homecomings one weekend after the next, but as the year went on our dances were overlapping and I decided to go back to his school because all of my friends were there. Also, when he picked me up at the Kansas house, the house had a staircase that led right down to the front door. When I was ready to go, I always tried to impress him by walking down the staircase like Cinderella. I was nervous every time I did it but I had fun doing it. We were apart for a year but made it work somehow.

For my sophomore year, I was back at his high school where I was meant to be in the first place. Both of us were happy to see each other every day. We went to every dance together and the dinner before the dance that the Special ED teachers put on for us. We had fun being in the same school again. I hoped it would never end.

In the summer before our junior year, I was at home with my mom and the phone rang. My mom picked it up and I knew something was wrong with my boyfriend. I just knew from the phone conversation that my boyfriend was coming to my house to breakup with me. When he came over I went outside with him with my big girl pants on. He told me that he loved me but he found another girlfriend that he loved. I was sad and held my crying back until he left. I couldn't believe that he found another girl that he loved even more than me. I cried for days but after a while I learned that we had nothing in common. I can't believe I just learned that after four years of dating him.

For my last two years of high school I didn't want to go to the dances. When the dances came around my mom wanted me to go get a dress. I told her that I didn't want to go but she told me that your girlfriends will be there and told me to go have fun. So I went to every dance and I had fun, but it was hard for me without my boyfriend. My mom helped me by telling me that we didn't have anything in common and told me that I am a strong woman. When I heard that it really helped.

In the summer of 2011 after I graduated from high school, someone else who I wasn't expecting asked me to go to the movies with him and another couple. I was speechless and I said yes. I couldn't believe it! I was going to see the last Harry Potter movie with a cuter boy then my last boyfriend. I thought it would be a onetime thing, because we only see each other at a play camp every summer and live far apart, but was shocked that he asks me out every year. Then we started to go out to eat alone after the performance and started learning about each other. I learned that we had more in common than I had with my ex-boyfriend. Every time we see each other we hug and catch up on what we have been up to over a year. Also, we hang out together as much as we can during our one week play camp. I always have fun hanging out with him.

I know that he is shy and he hasn't asked me to be his girlfriend yet but the signs are there that he loves me. When we go out to eat, he always buys for me and tells me that he would buy anything for me. We hold hands as we walk and dance together as much as we can.

Since I moved out to Snowmass I get to see him twice a year when he comes out to ski on his spring break. You know you are in love when he texts you and says he wants to meet up, and you are in a rush to change outfits as fast as you can and run out the door to meet him. We have been seeing each other for six years now and I know somewhere in my heart that he will ask me to be his girlfriend one day.

I am happy to have a friend that is a boy who has stuff in common with me and acts like a boyfriend before making it real. I will wait for him to ask me to be his girlfriend as long as it takes. When you are a woman with CP be open to anything that comes to you when you don't believe that you can find true love.

Snowmass Angel the Biography of Danielle Coulter

BONUS: If Dan Can Shred – You Can Too

www.dancanshred.com

"A #2 pencil and a dream can take you any where." ~ Joyce Meyer

Inspired by the book I, Win by Win Kelly Charles (Amazon)

Written By: Danielle Coulter

ACKNOWLEDGMENTS

I would like to thank these people for helping me make this book a reality. Without them this book will still be on my laptop or an idea still in my head.

First I would like to thank my mom, Sherilyn Tarver, for helping me to be the woman that I am today. I also want to thank her for translating my CP words into real words. (When you have CP you sound out words that sound right to your ear.) And a HUGE thanks for not stopping translating words because she said that it is so funny that she wanted to leave it. (Now I wish that I had two documents up and running of my book so I could save the unedited one so I can laugh again at what I did and share it with my friends, because me and my mom were laughing so hard.)

Thank you to my friend, Cathy Crum, for doing the second round of proof reading. She has taught me how to act since I was five years old and still helps out at the Magic of Music and Dance Camp. I always have fun working with her at camp every year. I was thrill that she offer to edit my book!

Thank you to my BFF, Win Charles. We met at the first Magic of Music and Dance

Camp and been best friends ever since. I don't know how I ever had writing this book without her good energy and encouragement everyday by text, email, Facebook, or Face

Time. Every time that I didn't feel in the mood to write I always think of her writing her next book every day, and it made me feel that I need to step up my game and I did. And a

HUGE last thanks for writing "I, Win" because that gave me a huge left up on writing my book. I thought if she could write a book then why can't I?

Thank you to my professional book editor and cover designer, Carla Wynn Hall, for editing my book in the final stages, the amazing book cover design that she did on this book, and being my PR Manager. I am really happy that Win introduced us! Thank you to my recorder, Joshua Adam Mancil, for recording my book into an audiobook. I am thrilled that my book is in an audiobook format, because people who have a disability who can't hold a book and read well can have the opportunity to listen to my story.

Thank you to my friend, Kathleen Kastner. As I was writing my book one of the books that I read was her book "The Cheerleader Speaks." (It can be found on amazon.com and

I highly recommend it to all women who want to find their sole mate.) As I was reading it I saw that at every beginning of each chapter there was a quote that go along with the chapter. I thought what a great idea and decided to do the same thing to make my book more powerful to go along with my chapters and pictures. Thanks for the inspiration! Last I want to thank all the people who kept pushing my buttons to write this book for many years, especially Kathy Quinn. I don't remember what she said but I know her words malted in my heart at the let of night when we were waiting to board an airplane to go to Ireland for The Elders tour. I'll never forget that moment or that trip with her.

RESUBMISISSION
Thank you, Rich Ganson, for helping me fix the technical stuff about skiing and snowboarding in Chapter Two and Three. I don't know what I would have done without your help. When I go out on Snowmass Mountain, I always have fun with you out on the
hill.

CHAPTER ONE
Growing Up In a Small Town

"There are only two ways to live your life. One is as though nothing is a miracle. The other is as though everything is a miracle."
~ Albert Einstein

My name is Danielle Coulter and I was born with Cerebral Palsy. I am writing this book about my life with all of my stories and adventures for you to read. I hope that after you read this book it will inspire you to stand up and follow your dreams whether you have a disability or not. Before I get into my story I just want to tell you that writing a book for the first time will be a huge adventure for me.

I was born in a house in a small town in Missouri called Parkville. My mom Sherilyn and my dad Mark wanted me to come into the world in my own home where I would grow up instead of in a hospital. Before I was born my mom was researching names to name me. She came up with two names- Tara and Nicole- but she realized that if she had named me Nicole it would be really hard to say with my last name. Try to say

Nicole Coulter five times in a row... See, I told you it would be hard. So she decided to call me Tara. Everything was going smoothly to get ready for me until my mom's midwife didn't come to the house the last two weeks before I came into my family's lives. At this point no one knew what I was going through but I knew.

When I was in my mom's tummy I was a wiggly worm. I love to move and roll over like a puppy. One day I rolled over too much. I realized my umbilical cord was around my neck and started to suffocate me. I realized that I had to do something fast to live, because I didn't want to die before I met my new family. I suddenly started moving my arm up to my neck and squeezed my arm up between my neck and my umbilical cord. I was so determined to live that I got my whole arm up through the free hole between the cord and my neck. Just then I realized that I had my arm stuck and I couldn't move it at all. I could only put my arm over my head. I had to stay like this until I came out into the world. I also knew that I would hurt myself and my mom when I came out, but I thought it would be better for us to be hurt together than having my mom be scarred for life.

Back outside my mom was worried the midwife wouldn't come back to help with the delivery so my mom called her sister Rebecca; soon to be my aunt. My aunt knew right away what to do because she did the same thing with my two oldest cousins and soon a third after me. My aunt called her best friend and midwife and asked her to help out and she said yes. She came and helped my mom get ready for me. On March 4, 1992 I decided it was time to see my mom and my family. When I let my mom know she let everyone know it was time to bring me in the world. My dad, aunt, and the new midwife were all there to help my mom and me out. It took a really long time for me to be born that it moved into the early morning.

My whole family didn't go to bed including my Granddad who was at his own house waiting for my arrival and wanted to be ready to wake up my grandma, Gran, so they could come right over and see me. In fact, Granddad had awakened and intuitively sensed something was wrong and started to send energy to Mom and me. I was born at

4:00 AM on March 5th. I couldn't breathe because the umbilical cord was wrapped around my neck. I later found out that I had brain damage, due to lack of oxygen, to the cerebellum and ganglia. One is responsible for balance and the other coordination. The midwife gave me CPR and my Mom and Dad were talking to me, telling me they loved me and wanted me to live. My dad quickly got scissors and cut the umbilical cord and after I got my breath back he put me into my mom's arms because she couldn't wait to see her new Tara. When my mom looked at my face she said, "You are not a Tara, you are a Danielle." When I heard that my name would be Danielle, I smiled.

My family knew that it would be a huge adventure for them and me. They wanted to help me to be as independent as I could. My mom started by taking me to be Rolfed when I was about six months old. I went to see Dr. Chopra when I was three, and received physical, occupational and speech therapy also when I was three. These all helped me be stronger and to move every part of my body on my own. I also attended preschool for two years to improve my motor and proprioception skills before I went to Kindergarten. I also got a walker when I was four so I could walk on my own, move my legs, and not be attached to my mom's hip all the time. My mom also put me in gymnastics and horseback riding to help me with my balance.

When I was five my mom entered me in the Platte County Fair's horse show. I was getting ready to go with my cowgirl hat, a white top with a vest and blue jeans, and my new pink cowgirl boots. When it was about show time my mom put me on my horse and we went into the arena. I felt really nervous because it was my first horse show, but

I knew what to do. I just had to listen and do what the judge told me to do, and smile all the time. I was doing fine until my boots began to fall off. I leaned over and pulled them up and went back to what I was doing, and hoped it wouldn't happen again, but it did. My boots keep falling off every five minutes and I pulled them up and just went right back on what I was doing, and I did this during the whole show. When it was time to line up to hear who won for each events I was really anxious that I wouldn't get a ribbon because of my boots. Every time that the judge announced the winner for each event I got even more anxious because I didn't hear my name yet. When the judge got to the Lead

Line event he announced, "And 1st place go to Danielle Coulter"! When I heard my name I was totally shocked that I won 1st place even with my boots falling off! I also won several trophies at Heartland Therapeutic Riding horse shows.

Over the years my mom let me take horseback riding lessons with her horse trainer, Cathy Huddleston. She is awesome to work with. She walked beside me so I won't fall and my mom would lead the horse. She helped me with everything from turning my house, gallop, and much more. Cathy even helped me get and train my own horse, Echo. Echo is a white and brown paint, and is seventeen hands tall. He had been trained to have dead side so if I hit his sides he won't go off run. Every time I work with Cathy and Echo I always have fun.

Once I finished preschool and had my Individualized Education Program (IEP) it was time for me to go to Kindergarten. An IEP is where kids with disabilities can get equipment and aids to help them with everything like writing for them or reading to them. I had a chair to help me sit well and tools to help me write and eat better. Also, I had an augmentative device that helped me communicate with my friends and my teachers but, I didn't want to have a machine talk for me.

I wanted to talk on my own. Over my elementary years I learned how to talk when someone couldn't understand me by using hand gestures and sign language. My speech teacher, Miss Reed, helped me to talk better to help me be understood. She would come into the classroom to teach sign language to my classmates and help them understand me. Later she put together a sign language club so anyone who wanted to learn the language could come. A lot of my friends and classmates came to learn with me so that they could understand me better when I needed to sign. Once Christmastime came around Miss Read started teaching us how to sign the song Jingle Bells. She saw we were all getting the hang of it and asked if we wanted to sign the song with the school's choir at our Christmas assembly and we all said yes. Miss Reed asked our music teacher if we could sign Jingle Bells while the choir was singing, and she said yes. When Miss Reed told us the music teacher said yes, my friends and I practiced every day after school, even when we didn't have sign language club, so we could be ready for the big day. Once the day arrived we had the signs to the song down pat. We were excited all day long and couldn't wait until it was time for the assembly. Once it was time to go down to the gym for the assembly, Miss Reed got me and everyone in the club seated in the front row so we could just jump up and sign away. When the assembly began our principal read the book The Night before Christmas; everybody loved it.

After the story was over, it was time for the choir to sing Christmas songs. When it was time for the choir to sing Jingle Bells the music teacher announced us as we lined up in a row so everybody could see us. Once the music began we all knew what to do. As I was listening and signing to the song I had the biggest smile on my face because I also was thinking how cool it was to show other kids there is another way to communicate without using your voice. When we were done the whole school was whooping and hollering. When I heard that, it made me feel really good.

My mom and dad were really supportive of me when I was going through school. They helped me study, asked me questions to get me ready for tests, and helped me in any way to get my reading level up. When I got to be a sophomore in high school my mom fought for me to be in regular classes with everybody else and not be in the Special

Ed class anymore, because she knew that I was smart enough to be in a regular class.

My mom got me in all regular classes except I still had to be in Special Ed Language Arts, P.E., Reading 180, and speech therapy. I was really happy that my mom did this for me because I could be with everybody else and be in different classrooms with different kids and not in the same classroom all day long with the same kids. My mom also supported me in horseback riding, and helped my muscles to relax by getting me massages every week because my muscles where always on and they wouldn't relax.

It was so bad that my feet started to turn in and I had to get braces to walk normally.

My dad is into sports and magic. He always takes me to the Kansas City Royals baseball and Chiefs football games as many times as he can. I always have fun going with him to watch the games. He also has club tickets for both Royals and Chiefs so I can eat as much as I want to in both of the clubs. One year I got into the Royal's Kid Club and I got to run the bases with my walker after a game; that was so cool! He also loves to watch magic on TV and in person. He saw that I was scared to watch magic and when he watched it I couldn't even be around him.

My dad wanted to show me that magic was cool, so one night he took me to a pizza restaurant in my home town that is called Stone Canyon Pizza to meet his magic friend named Gene to show me some sleight of hand. Gene showed me some cool magic tricks like card tricks, how to grow a penny as big as a hand, and how to turn an old piece of chewed up gum into a new one that hasn't even been unwrapped. He also asked me to help him when he got three red balls out of his invisible bag. He told dad and I to squeeze a ball in our hands. He told me that he would make my dad's ball hit my drinking glass and go into my hand with the ball that I was holding. He then said some magic words and told me to open my hand. When I did I saw that he had two balls and I looked at my dad's hand when he opened it he didn't have his ball.

Gene started moving the balls some more and by the end of the trick I had all three balls in my hand. I thought that was so cool! By the end of the night I told my dad that I really liked Gene's magic tricks and I wanted to go back again next week. So we went back the next week and many other times. Soon Gene and my dad got me some magic kits that would be easy for me to do because my hands were not steady enough to do the type of magic tricks Gene does. I practiced a lot at home and soon got the hang of

it.

After I knew what I was doing I showed some tricks to my friend Chelsea and soon we decided that we wanted to do a magic act in our school talent show. We made up magic tricks to do together and alone.

We practiced a lot. Chelsea's mom made top hats and capes for us to wear in the show. The night of the show, Chelsea and I were in the bathroom getting ready for the show, with both of our moms helping us. We both looked like real magicians with white tops, white gloves, black pants, and our home-made top hats and capes. To top our outfits off, Chelsea's mom pinned red roses on our tops and painted back mustaches on our faces.

While the show was going on we asked our friends to come on stage and help with a trick, and they said yes. When it was our turn we just went out there and had a blast. We had so much fun that we wanted to audition for the talent show the next year. We worked really hard to make a new magic act with all new tricks. We brought in

Chelsea's sister, Haley, into the act as our assistant. We also wanted to make the act funny, so we got a big cardboard box and wrote Magic Box on it. We put all of our magic tricks and Haley in. Our plan was to have the magic box with our magic tricks and Haley in it already on stage while Chelsea and I were backstage.

When our act began we would walk out onstage and Chelsea would say, "There is our magic box, but where is our lovely assistant?" and Haley would jump up out of the box and say, "Here I am!" and scare us, then we would start to do our tricks. We practiced day and night on getting our act down for the talent show auditions. When the day to audition came we were all ready to go.

When it was time to go to our audition we got all of our stuff and ran to get Haley because she was one grade below us. We then went to the lunch room and got everything setup onstage for our act. After we did our act in front of the teachers, they said it was too long and we went over the time limit; we didn't make the cut to be in the talent show.

We were sad and mad that we worked so hard on the act and we didn't do a magic act for the talent show for the rest of our elementary years.

When I was in 7th grade I saw that the school was holding talent show auditions and I decided I wanted to do a magic act all by myself. When my dad picked me up from school I told him that the school was holding talent show auditions and I wanted to do a magic act in the show. He liked the idea and started to help me get together some magic tricks that I already had. I practiced a lot to see what was the best way to perform each trick. Finally, I had every trick down the night before the audition.

The next day after school my dad came with all of my magic tricks and watched my audition. The person who was holding the auditions was my friend Chris' dad. When it was time to audition I was a little nervous but I was ready to do my stuff. After I was done, Chris' dad said that he really loved it and I was in. I was so excited because I had done a magic act all by myself and I didn't even mess up once. When the day of the talent show came I was happy all day at school and couldn't wait for the talent show that night. My day was going great until I got home.

When I got home my dad surprised me with a brand new magic trick. He went to buy it while I was in school and thought it would be a huge ending to my act. It was a huge magic trick that takes strength and steady hands to do it. The trick was a colorful box that had a window on the front and a yellow cylinder inside of it. He demonstrated it to me. He picked up the box and showed me that it was hollow and nothing was in it, then put it back down on the black platform with the cylinder in the middle. Next, he did the same thing with the cylinder, then put his hand inside of the cylinder and pulled out a huge magic cane that was two times as tall as I was! I was shocked at how that huge cane came out of the little cylinder.

After he showed me the trick he showed me how it worked. Next, I tried to do it and massed up a lot. I told my dad that I couldn't learn this trick in four hours before the show, but he kept on pushing me and said that I could do it. So I kept working on it and my dad added a paper bag to put the cane in so it would make it easier for me to pull the bag out of the cylinder, and then pull the cane out of the bag. After about two hours I got the trick down and my dad and I added one more thing to the trick to top it all off. We added a yellow scarf that turned into a medium sized cane. So my plan was to pull out the scarf first and pop that into the medium sized cane, and then the paper bag with the huge cane in it to make it cooler and funnier. I was so excited that I would be able to do the trick and have a big finale for my magic act at the show that night.

When I got to the high school where they were holding the talent show I was happy they were doing a run through before the real show, so I could practice my magic act: including the new trick one more time. My dad helped set up all of my tricks before my last practice. When it was about time for my run through I shook out my hands so they could be looser so I could do my tricks, but mostly for my huge magic trick. After I did the run through I felt really good because I didn't mess up, and my dad helped setup everything again for the real show.

While the show was going on I sat down backstage and talked with my friends, and tried to relax. When the act before me went on I started to shake out my hands again to get them ready for show time. When the act was done my friends helped me bring out two chairs; one for me and one for my little tricks so I could reach them. I was so nervous but after I did my first trick my nerves just went away. After I did all of my little tricks it was time for my huge trick. My dad was in the front row so he could slide the box to me and put it between my feet. When I saw it was coming to me I was nervous again and I shook out my hands again before I began the trick.

After I showed everybody the box and the cylinder was empty, I put my hand into the cylinder to start to pull out the yellow scarf. When the announcer saw that I had my hand in the cylinder he got way excited and started to announce what I was pulling out like at a basketball game. When I pulled out the scarf everybody clapped and when I

popped it into a cane they went wild. Then the announcer thought I was done and started to thanks me for my magic act, but when he saw my hand going back into the cylinder he yelled, "Wait, "What is she getting now? It's a bag!" Everybody got wilder, and then I opened up the bag and started to pull out the huge cane. While I was pulling it out it messed up a little bit and I fixed it, but I didn't care because everybody went wilder. After I bowed and I went backstage, I went wild, because I did a magic act all by myself and I didn't give up on myself doing the new magic trick my dad got me that day. My dad was proud of me and I was, too.

The next year I did the same act, but this time my dad and Chris' dad asked if Chris could help me so it would be easier. We both said yes. We had so much fun working together, and I am thankful to have him as a friend. We also did the magic act at our last day of school's assembly as well as our last middle school day. It was so cool. I am so glad my dad showed me that magic is cool, but you still won't see me around

magic tricks that deal with people and sharp things.

One more thing that is cool about my dad is when I was young he always took my cousins and me to a rock climbing gym to work on our strength, coordination, teamwork, and just to have a fun time. We helped each other out by calling out the next move to whoever is climbing up the rock wall at the time, and we cheered them on. When it was my turn to climb all of the men had to help pull me up, because I didn't have enough strength to hold my body weight by myself, but I tried my best and did most of the work. Every time I got up I get stronger and get better at where I put my hands and feet to get up to the top of the wall.

I became more aware of where my body was. Before I got up the wall I would think that I would get to the top and usually I did. Over my elementary school years I got better and better at rock climbing. One day my dad decided to donate a rock wall to my school gym so other kids could rock climb, too. When my friends and I heard about this we thought my dad was the coolest dad ever.

When the wall finally got built my gym teacher let my dad know when the first day that my class was going to use it so he could be there to see my friends and I climb the wall. My classmates and I set down on the gym floor in our normal spots to wait for the gym teacher. When I sat down I looked toward the door to see if my dad was coming and I saw that he was talking to the teacher. When they were done talking, they came into the gym, and the teacher started to tell us about the wall and that my dad donated it. My dad was standing behind us.

After she was done talking she asked me if I would like to be the first one and show my friends how to climb the wall and I said yes. Before I hopped on the wall she told me that you have to go sideways, and she had to hold me up because there was no harness. I had never done a sideway rock wall so this was a new experience for me. She picked me up and I started to climb sideways. All of my friends started to cheer me on and were yelling what move I should make next. Finally, I made it all the way across the wall and everybody went wild. The teacher then spotted my friends as they climbed across the rock wall. We cheered everybody on as they climbed the rock wall.

Looking back, I am happy that my dad donated that rock wall to help able-

bodied kids to rock climb.

CHAPTER TWO

A Normal Day Turns Into a "Challenge Aspen Day"

"I may not have gone where I intended to go, but I think I have ended up where I needed to be." ~ Douglas Adams, "The Long Dark Tea-Time of the Soul"

Since the 1980's my family has been vacationing in Snowmass, Colorado. They have always taken me to Snowmass in the summer and winter times. I remember when my family went on hikes in the summer, my mom always carried me and I could see everything the mountain's nature has to offer. When my mom got tired of carrying me she put me in the baby carrier on my dad's back. I always liked to ride on my dad's back, because I was up higher and I could see more. Today as an adult, I still love to be up high on top of a mountain so I can see everything from the sunrise to the sunset.

A couple of years later when I was five years old, I was walking with my mom in my walker in the Snowmass Mall on a lovely summer afternoon. We were on our way to go to the car to go home for the day. On the way we saw a lady came wheeling up to us in her wheelchair. She introduced herself as Amanda Boxtel and asked me if I had ever skied before and I said "no". Amanda said, "Do you want to?" and I said "yes". I was four and I learned I could begin ski lessons when I turned five on March 5th the following year.

She then told us to follow her up to Challenge Aspen's office to get signed up to go skiing. As my mom and I were following her we were thinking that this was awesome.

When we got to the office my eyes got wider, because I couldn't believe what was happening. Amanda introduced us to everybody, and they were excited to meet us.

Amanda right away asked for the ski papers so my mom could fill them out. While my mom was filling the papers out Amanda was talking about summer camps and other stuff that Challenge Aspen had to offer. One was an art camp and the other was a new Music and Dance camp that they were putting together for the up-coming summer. My mom asked if I would like to do the camps also and I yelled "YES" with a big grin on my face.

It seemed like my first day of skiing would never come but finally one day in

March it did. A ski teacher named Rich Ganson met us at the Big Burn Bears Ski School. Before we went to get my ski boots and skis, Rich and I set down on a bench to chat for a while. When he asked me when my birthday was, I said, "March 5th', then he said, "No way, are you kidding? Mine is too!" We were both shocked and thought that was so awesome. After we talked we went to rent my ski boots and skis from the ski rental place, then went back to the ski school to try to figure out how I would be able to ski. The issue was that CA only had a squawker for a disabled kid who could walk with a walker. This day was really important in my life.

Once I got into my skis and the squawker, Rich put a rubber band called an edgy wedgy onto my ski tips. Rich then realized that the squawker didn't give me the support I needed. He cut one of his ski poles and made the spreader bar with a bungee cord and large washers to put in-between my boots so they wouldn't come apart and make me do the splits or fall down while I was skiing. Next, Rich put tethers on the back so he could hold me and help me turn when I needed it. Before we got on the hill he taught me the French fries and pizza ski moves. The French fries move is when you have your skis straight and you go fast. The pizza move is when you slide your heals apart and you keep the front of your ski tips together to help to slow down and stop. When I got the moves down it was time to do my first ski run of my life. Rich took me out of the squawker and we took everything outside to the hill to get ready to go.

When we got everything out there and got dialed in it was time to go down the hill. When we were going downhill I was listening to Rich and tried my best to do what he told me to do. While I was listening to Rich, I took everything in that I could see, and was thinking that wasn't real but it was. I love having the wind in my face when I am going fast. When we got down the hill I was so excited that I did my first ski run ever and I wanted to ski more. Next, Rich showed me how to get on the chairlift to ride up the mountain to ski down again. I was scared that I was going to miss the chair and fall down, but Rich and the chairlift staff helped me get on the chair and that was a relief for me.

On the way up the mountain I could see all of the skiers going down the hill and some going off jumps, going through the half pipe, and some even racing each other in the racecourse. I thought that was way cool. Then I saw a pond that had five crocodiles heads popping out of the snow and Rich told me that their names where Eny, Meeny, Miney, Moe, and Big Fat Joe. I laughed at that and every time that we passed them we both yelled their names together and laughed. Then I saw the top of the chairlift where we got off. Rich told me that I had to keep my ski tips up so I wouldn't fall down or lose my skis. I was scared, but I kept my ski tips up and made it. I was scared of the chairlift but after I rode it a million times and lost my skis a lot I got used to it.

At that time we were only on Fanny Hill because I was learning the ropes of skiing. But I knew I would be skiing more hills on Snowmass Mountain in no time. The next year we realized the squawker was holding me back and Challenge Aspen had nothing else to offer. Rich knew that he could use outriggers, which CA did have, but he would need to add cross support to stabilize it all. (Outriggers are like ski poles but they have skis on the bottom of them.) Rich cut another ski pole and used bungee cords to create a semi-solid frame for more support.

The next couple of years CA bought a slider called Ski Legs that was made by a company called Yetti. It was like my semi-solid, but it was a lot stronger, made out of metal and had armrests for my arms. It had it's own full -length skis. When I was in the slider I was going faster than when I was in the semi-solid. I was going so fast my family couldn't keep up and started calling me Avalanche. I got to go off little jumps and go on buffalo bumps, which were my favorites.

Rich took me everywhere on the mountain, and on every kid's trail. My two favorite kid's trails were through the woods with a lot of bumps and turns, and one where you go down a curvy path and end up by a fence where you can see real reindeer. Sometimes the reindeer came up to me and I got to pet them. I thought that was so cool. I had a blast skiing with Rich all week long and I didn't want it to end.

Also, I got to ski with ski racers from all over the world. Aspen used to hold an event called 24 Hours of Aspen. The 24 Hours of Aspen was a ski race where the best ski racers from all around the came together to race for 24 hours on Aspen Mountain. There were two people to a team so you had a mate to watch your back, and to help each other out. Two days before the day of the race, Challenge Aspen had a day where the racers could come ski with the disabled skiers and try out the equipment to see how it feels to be disabled. I was happy to be a part of this event and meet all of the ski teams from different countries.

"The pressure people put on themselves and the rivalry between the teams is much more marked. And I think that's a good thing. As long as that rivalry remains within the spirit of competition, it con only spur everyone on." ~ Eric Cantona

Each of Challenge Aspen's participants got teamed up with a ski team to ski with for the day. I got teamed up with a lot of good teams over the years. One year I got teamed up with brothers who were twins. One year my ski team was from Ireland and Switzerland. I had fun showing them how I skied, skiing with and talking to the teams every year. I thought that was so cool. When the races were going on I would turn on the TV to see how my team was doing and root for them.

One time my dad took me to Aspen Mountain to watch the race live. We went to wait in line to get on to the gondola to get to the top of the mountain to see the race from down below. When we got to Aspen Mountain the base of the mountain was loud from the race, packed with people and there were tents where people could buy food and souvenirs. We had to wait in a huge line to ride the gondola because a lot of people had the same idea. We had to wait and let the racers go first so they could keep racing and have their best time.

When we got up closer to the Gondola, I could see everything that was going on.

All of Gondola staff were moving fast by putting the racers' skis in the ski holders on the gondola and moving shopping carts that were full of food and blankets, back and forth, for the racers to have on their ride up the mountain. I was amazed how fast they were going; they looked like chickens with their heads chopped off. As I was watching, the line was getting shorter and I was glad it was almost time for my dad and me to get into the gondola because I was freezing and couldn't wait to get into the gondola and get warm.

When it was finally our turn to get into the gondola we had to run and dodge the staff that was running around and hopped into the gondola because they wouldn't slow it down because of the race. When we got in and the doors closed it was warmer and my dad started rubbing my hands to warm them up. As we were riding up the mountain it was really cool to see the mountain at nighttime; the Aspen city's buildings all lit up and all of the racers zipping down the racecourse below us.

When we got to the top we had to do the same thing as we did at the bottom of the gondola. When we got out we had to hurry to the fans' box where the people were watching the race so the staff who were working on top could have room to hurry and get the skis out of the ski holders and put them down on the edge of the hill before the racers got out of the gondola so the racers could just run out and snap into their skis and go down the mountain at the speed of lightening.

My dad got me right in front of the fans' box so I could see the racers flash in and out in front of my own eyes. I could only see what they had on when they snapped into their skis for about three seconds, then they skied into a blur down the hill and around a corner, then they disappeared. I saw a team go down the hill every ten seconds. I was amazed how fast that they were going. I had so much fun watching the race from the top of the mountain with my dad that night even though I was freezing.

Another year, Amanda asked me if I would love to pull out the winning ticket for the lucky person who would win a Jeep at the awards ceremony the next morning when the 24 Hours of Aspen race was over, and I said yes. So this meant that I had to get up really early and be at the bottom of Aspen Mountain before 9:00 AM; before the racers skied in from their last run. The night before I was really excited about what I would be doing the next morning and I went to bed really early so I could be at the bottom of the mountain before 9:00.

The next morning my mom and I hurried to get ready to go and we met Amanda at the awards stage at 8:30. I was excited that Amanda asked me to do this. We had to wait for the racers to come down from their last run of the race. Everybody was dead silent waiting to see the racers coming down the hill. When they saw the racers everybody went up in an uproar. I was yelling, too, even though I could barely see the racers because of the brightness of the morning sun. Then a man told us to move back because we were right in the middle of where the racers would ski in and run up on stage. We moved back and then the racers came skiing in and ran up on stage in front of my own eyes. I was amazed.

After all of the team got on stage the Master of Ceremonies (MC) started the show. After the MC talked about how hard these racers train for this 24 Hours race he announced Amanda and me. He asked us up on stage to draw the ticket that had the lucky person's name who would win a new Jeep. My mom put me on Amanda's lap and then we rolled up on stage.

While the MC announced us and what I would be doing I saw all the video
cameras and cameras flashes going off in my face. Next, the MC held a huge glass bowl with a lot of tickets inside in front of me. The

crowd roared as I put my arm in the bowl and started to mix up the tickets really good before I pulled out the lucky ticket. When I pulled out the ticket I gave it to the MC so he could read the ticket's number out loud. He read the number out loud like ten times and no one responded that they had that number. He then looked to see if there was a name and a cell phone number on the ticket and there was.

The MC dialed the number to see if he could get ahold of the person to tell them they had won the jeep and he did. The person on the phone went crazy that they won and everyone else went crazy, too. After he got off the phone it was time to give out medals to the racers and I was lucky enough to watch the awards ceremony while I was still on stage with Amanda. The staff gave Champagne bottles to the racers. The MC told us to get off the stage because he didn't want us to be sprayed. I didn't know what that meant, but we got off stage and then turned around to see what was about to happen. The racers shook up the Champagne bottles really well, then the MC said, "One... Two... Three..." At three the racers opened up their Champagne bottles and started spraying each other. Everybody went crazy to see this, and I was amazed and shocked at what happened in front of me at first, then I started to laugh. That was the best day that I had with Amanda.

The next year was even better because I was on the sideline again with Amanda and one of my Challenge Aspen friends named Amy. Amy was going to do the same thing that I did, and I was happy for her. I got to watch Amy and Amanda from the sideline. That was pretty special for me to watch my friend do the same thing that I did.

CHAPTER THREE

A Little Video Game Turns Into a Huge Deal

"Our deepest fear is not that we are inadequate, our deepest fear, is that we are powerful beyond measure." ~ Marianne Williamson

The Christmas of 2000 my family and I were in Snowmass. We had a huge

Christmas dinner in my grandparents' log house in Snowmass Village. After we ate it was time to open presents and my cousins and I got a lot of great things, but my favorite was a Play Station 2 with a lot of video games from my dad. One of the games was a snowboarding game that is called SSX Tricky. That night my dad helped set up the PS2 in the TV den so my cousins Zac, Elliott, and I could start playing the games.

Over time I learned my favorite game was SSX Tricky. Over that year I played that game as much as I could and sometimes I asked my mom if she wanted to race me and she said, "Yes, but only one race." When we finished a race she always wanted to race again to see if she could beat me, but she couldn't beat me. We loved the game so much that we started to sing the main chorus in the game theme, "It's Tricky, It's Tricky,

It's Really, Really Tricky!"

The next December when I was nine years old, my family and I came out to Snowmass to ski and Zac started to snowboard. I had fun watching him while I was in my slider and I wanted to tell Rich that I played a snowboard video game at home. So one day we all went to

Brothers' Grille to eat lunch. I thought this was the perfect time to tell Rich.

Hold up, I have to jump out of my story for a minute because I have to tell you

one of my Cerebral Palsy challenges I had back then. While I was thinking about what I want to say, I couldn't get the words out all the way and little bits and pieces would come out of my mouth. I wanted to tell Rich that I played a snowboard video game at home, but all that came out of my mouth was "I snowboard". You will see that what I thought was a "booboo" was really an invitation for me to do more.

"No, you don't," Rich replied, "You have never snowboarded with me." Then my dad had to jump in and tell Rich about the video game that I got last Christmas. When my dad got done with the story Rich said, "But why not? Why can't Danielle snowboard in real life? We can make it happen." Then I was, like, wow, did he really say that?

My accidental word flub started a hurricane. I was going to snowboard in real life! Now I was really excited. Right after lunch Rich grabbed my arm to go to stores in the mall to get snowboard gear. He was so excited that he started to run, and I tried my best to keep up, but mostly he was dragging me. We went to every sport store in the mall.

Every time when we got into a store, Rich yelled, "This nine year old disability girl wants to snowboard!" Every worker knew Rich and started to grab all the stuff we needed from

left and right.

They even ran it up to the counter so we didn't have to move around. My family started to pull out money to pay for the gear, but every store wanted to donate everything to Challenge Aspen, because they wanted me to snowboard and they had never heard that there was any adaptive snowboards in the whole wide world. My eyes got so wide on what was happening in front of me and it was amazing. Then when we had everything we ran to the Challenge Aspen office so Rich could tell everyone what just happened.

Everybody was excited for me, and then Rich called his friend, Bobby Palm, to tell him I wanted to snowboard and ask him to help build an adaptive snowboard. Bobby said,

"Yes, let's start it today so Danielle can be on it tomorrow!" Bobby had already been working on a first version of the snowboard that he came up with. He had planned to use it with some students he had, but timing of Rich and me being the dreamer was perfect and my desires gave us the opportunity to really try it out first! When Rich got off the phone he told us what Bobby had said, and Rich told us to be in the Challenge Aspen's equipment room at 9 o'clock tomorrow morning so we could get the snowboard ready to go out on the hill. I was so excited that I couldn't even bare it.

That night I could hardly sleep because I was too excited about snowboarding in real life and not just in my SSX Tricky world at home any more. The next morning when I went into the equipment room I saw Rich and Bobby working on the board. Rich introduced Bobby to my family and me, then they showed me what they did to the snowboard we had gotten the day before. The snowboard now had a bar made out of PVC pipe that came up in front of and from behind the two-foot plates, which are the snowboard bindings, and across my belly line. The top bar was at an angle so Rich could hold on to one side and help me. I thought this was so awesome. After they showed it to me it was time for me to get into the snowboard and get everything right; like how far away my legs needed to be from each other. When we got my snowboard bindings in the right spots Rich realized I needed a seat so I wouldn't fall down when I went into my heel turn.

He got a rope, a pad, and duct tape and made a butt sling for me and tied it to both sides of the PVC pipe. Finally, Rich showed me how to do the snowboard moves; the toe turn and the heel turn. He told me that snowboarding was way different from skiing.

When you are snowboarding you have to go sideways and turn with your body weight from your toe to heal and vice-versa. When you are on your heel turn you have your butt out and when you are on your toe turn you have to have your butt in. It was hard for me because I used my whole upper body to move on to my toe and heel side, and I didn't use my legs. It took me some time to use my legs to turn and not use my upper body. When I got the moves down it was finally time to take the first adaptive snowboard in the world out on the hill. The little wiggly worm that was in my mom's tummy was about to make history.

When we were on the hill getting ready to go I felt way excited to do my first snowboard run. When we started down the hill I listened to Rich on which way to turn, and I was thinking that this is way easer and cooler then skiing. When we got down to the chair lift everyone was looking and asking about the snowboard and me. Rich told them that this is Danielle "Avalanche" Coulter and she is the first adaptive snowboarder. I liked the sound of that. When we got to the top we went on all the kid's trails, did little jumps, and buffalo bumps. When everybody saw us coming they stopped in awe, and I thought that was pretty cool. We also went through the trees and did 360s whenever we could and that was really fun. I also did the racecourse and the half pipe for the first time. Every time I went in the half pipe I wanted to go higher and higher because I love to fly high. (A half pipe is made of two big walls of snow that are parallel from each other so skiers and snowboarders can drop in from the top of one wall to go up the other wall and then turn around and repeat.)

One day I saw a huge jump; the biggest one in my life. I asked Rich what was the name of the jump, and he said it is a black diamond jump. I asked if I can go off the jump, and he said, "If you want to do it I am in." I said yes and we went down to the edge of the hill where you drop in to do the jump. My dad went down on the hill by lip of the jump to take a picture of me going off the jump. When my dad was ready we went down the hill…

Hold up and stop the story. You may be thinking that I was crazy, insane, and a dare devil. And you'd be right. Here is a story on how I became a dare devil when I was five years old. One sunny day I was riding my blue and rainbow toy horse around the Parkville house while my mom was cleaning. My mom took down the baby gate to clean the stairs. Suddenly, the phone rang and mom went to answer the phone. I saw that the gate was down and mom was in the kitchen on the phone. I thought that this would be a good time to have some fun. I rode my horse very quietly to the stairs so my mom wouldn't hear me. Then I turned my horse and lined him up on top of the stairs. I looked back to see if my mom saw me but she had her back towards me still talking on the phone.

I was worried that she would see and stop me but she didn't, and I was happy about that. Then I turned back around and got ready for a ride of a lifetime. I tightened my hand on my handles on my horse's head, then I pushed off with my feet. On the way down I was bumping up and down. I was having a blast, then my mom heard the big banging and turned around to see what it was. When she saw it was me riding my horse down the stairs, she yelled, throwing her arms up and flinging the phone in the air. She ran to see if I was okay. When she got to the top of the stairs she was relieved to see I was on the landing on my horse up right and laughing. That was my story on how I

became a dare devil, and now back to the black diamond jump...

Now, where was I?, oh yeah. We were about to go off the black diamond jump. After my dad gave us the thumbs up that he was ready to take the picture, it was time for us to take off. We took off down the hill picking up speed, and I felt like a jet just getting ready to take off into the air. When we went off the jump we went way high and caught too much air. So much, it made us go way higher than my dad's head. We were like 10 feet into the air and I know that we were both thinking holy moly. We tried to make our landing good and hoped we would make it. The PVC pipe was brittle on that cold day and even though we landed well the PVC shattered and I fell on my back and the PVC pipe came off my board and hit my jaw. My dad yelled down to Rich, "Rich, is she ok?"

Rich yelled back, "I will know after she is done laughing."

After I laughed my head off, Rich asked me if I was ok, and I said yes. My dad saw snowboarders up on the hill that wanted to go off the jump, and my dad went to the middle of the jump and waved to them to tell them to not go yet. The snowboarders saw him and got the message, but they could only see my dad's head and arms waving in the air. Rich moved me to the side of the hill out of the way of the jump so the snowboarders could jump and had my dad come down to us. Rich then check me out to see if I was ok and see if I had any broken bones in my body. I was fine, but I was cold. Yes, it was a cold day that made the pipe too brittle for the jump!

Rich asked my mom and dad to ski down to the ski school with my snowboard parts while he skied with me in his arms. When we got down the hill and into the school Rich gave me hot chocolate to warm me up, then we had lunch and fixed up my snowboard to have more fun in the afternoon. What I did that day was awesome, and I was happy that I survived and did that jump, but I won't do that jump again. To everyone who is reading this that has ever been afraid to take a chance because of a disability, don't be afraid. Fun is so fun.

The same week we spent a lot of time developing the snowboard so that it was fully functional and more adaptive for different needs and sizes. We changed the seat pad and the adjustable handlebar came a year or two later. Once we had added the various changes and parts to the board, it was taken to a great adaptive equipment company called Freedom Factory; they then built a version for all kids - and adults too - with challenges to be able to explore snowboarding. This new version was used for the first group of Iraqi war vets who came to Snowmass for rehabilitation and was a huge part of their growth. Some of this can be seen in the documentary "Beyond Iraq" which received accolades at the Sundance Film Festival. Who would have ever known that an adaptive snowboard would help veterans?

The next year I got to ride a snowboard with a bar that was made out of metal and it was stronger for a tough girl like me. Rich made his third version of a handle for him to hold on to so he could better control the rig. This was before the Freedom Factory made handle bars for the teachers. Rich also asked his friend, Vance, to come shoot a video of us on the snowboard to share what was happening in Snowmass with other states and countries around the world. Vance agreed and got a team together so we could get different shots from different angles. We had so much fun making the video with all the things we loved to do.

One sunny afternoon Vance and his team thought it was a perfect time to take some shoots of Rich and me in the racecourse. When we got up to the racecourse everyone went down to different spots on the racecourse to shoot, and even my dad went down to the bottom to take pictures. Rich and I got into a race box to get ready to go. In the box Rich told me that I had to turn right away when he said to make sharp turns, and if I didn't something would be bound to go wrong.

I felt nervous inside but I knew I could do this. Then a man came by and asked us if we were ready to go, and we said yes. Next, the man yelled, "On your mark, get set, go!" We flew out like a rocket ship. When Rich started calling out turns to me I did them, but it was intense. We were doing fine until on one of my heel turns Rich's uphill ski slid down under my snowboard and we started to fall. I didn't know what was happening, but all I knew was I bouncing around in a winter wonderland all alone with no sign of Rich, just snow all around me. I hoped that I would get out of there alive and I hoped Rich would, too. After about 10 seconds I was on my back and I could see the blue sky again. I started to laugh and I saw Rich coming up the hill to see if I was ok. Then he pulled me up onto my feet. After I got up I saw a camera was right in our faces, and Rich said,

"Well folks, we made it through that one." After that big explosion we called it a day.

When we got down to the mall I asked Vance if I could see the video because I wanted to see what my dad saw, because when he told me what he saw, I thought it was awesome, and I want to see it for myself. Vance said yes and told me and my dad to come by the office after we packed up for the day. He gave us the address so we knew how to get there. When we were packed up and into the car we went to the office to see the video. When we got inside the door everyone said hi to me and put me into an office chair and showed me around the office by pushing me in the chair. They had a lot of TVs, computers, and a camera equipment to make videos. They put me in the middle of the room in front of a huge TV. Vance said, "Now you are in the hot spot, because you are our star. Are you ready to see the video?" I yelled, "Yes!"

Vance put the video into a slot so it could play on the huge TV, then he hit play. The video was cool to watch on the big screen. I saw Rich and me coming down the race course in a shadow because the bright sun was behind us. We were ripping it up, and then when we got down farther and I could see our profiles better when we got out of the sun.

Then suddenly I saw Rich's upper ski go under my snowboard, then the video paused. Vance paused the video because he wanted to show my dad what had happened, and after they were done talking about it, Vance hit play again. When he hit play we fell and somehow our fall made all of the snow all around us go up like 20 feet into the air. The sun behind the show made it look like a huge sparkling snow globe. The camera zoomed in on where we were. It looked like we were in an avalanche.

I could only see myself, but not Rich, and I could only see parts of my body going in and out of the snow. When I did see myself, I looked like a rag doll, and at one point one of my arms hit and bounced off of a race gate pole like a doll arm. Then the avalanche went away and I could see myself on the ground. Rich picked me up and talked into the camera. After that Vance turned off the video and talked to us. He said that this video clip is so scary that he had to cut it out because the video is an inspirational video to show people what is happening in Snowmass. I understood, but I didn't want him to cut it out, because it was so awesome. I wanted to show it to my friends back home in Parkville. I knew I wouldn't see the video again, but I am happy that I shared this story with you in this book.

Here is a funny story about my dad that I just have to put in here. While I was snowboarding with my family one year we ran into another girl who skied with Challenge Aspen and we also met the person who was skiing with her, and her name was

Amy Grant. The girl was a big fan of Amy's and she emailed her to ask Amy to come out to ski with her, and Amy did. The girl asked me if I would like to ski with her and be in her video, and I said yes. So I got to ski with her and Amy for a day. It was so much fun.

At one of our rest stops, Amy said, "I know a perfect song to put into the video, but I forgot the name, but it goes a little like this." She starts singing the song, and she sang so beautifully that it amazed me and everybody else. When my family and I got back into

Parkville, my dad got back into the office and told he secretary, Ellen, this story. He said,

"Her voice sounded amazing." Then Ellen said, "I hope you didn't tell her that she should sing for a living." He said, "I was thinking about it." She said, "She won nine

Grammies." My dad didn't know who Amy was with all of the ski gear on. When he told me what happened at the office I laughed. That is the funny story about my dad, and how I met Amy Grant.

One year, Rich wanted me to try to ride a normal snowboard without the bar or anything. I was scared but I wanted to try. On the first day it was only Rich and me, and we were both on snowboards. We held hands and tried to snowboard together, but we fell every five seconds. It was like a circus act in Barnum and Bailey's. It was really hard and every time I fell, I fell the wrong way and I twisted my ankles. It hurt really badly. I told Rich I wanted to go back to my old snowboard.

Rich told me that if I stayed in there for three more days I would earn a whole day in the bi-ski on the last day. Yeah, I loved to go bi-skiing when my legs got tired from snowboarding. A bi-ski is a bucket set on skis for people who can't walk, and they get to ride in it while their teacher pushes them. I agreed to his bribe. The next day we got a buddy to help on my backside.

I also got a ring to wear on my waist so Rich and the buddy held on to it. It made it easier on all of us. Every day I got better and better. By the end of the last day of snowboarding I felt really proud of myself that I stayed in there even though I didn't want to do it. The next day was all fun in the bi-ski. I love to ride in the bi-ski because we go really fast. For example, one time when I was little my family, Rich, and I went to the top of Snowmass Mountain to end a perfect day of skiing. I told Rich I really wanted to do the half pipe one more time. Rich looked at his watch and told me that the lift closed in

15 minutes. He asked me, "Do you really want to do the half pipe?" I said, "Yes."

Then Rich told everybody what I wanted to do, and that we would meet my family at the mall because they weren't as fast as us. Then we turned around and went down the mountain as fast as lighting and made it the bottom of the mountain before the lift closed. I got to go into the half pipe again. Another fast and crazy experience, one year Rich had an iPhone app that could tell you how fast you are going.

Rich and I wanted to know how fast we could go on my snowboard. Our top speed was 32 miles per hour, and going at that speed we ended up falling on top of each other very near the trees. That's how crazy we are about going fast. The faster we went the more fun we had. A lot of the time when we were out on the hill we were not falling down. We had fun carving the hill and sometimes I got so deep into my turns that I hung my arms and almost touched the snow. Every time when I could almost touch the snow, I felt like a bird that has grace. It is an amazing feeling.

Last winter, when we were out on the hill, on a really snowy day, all that week

Snowmass got a ton of snow and it was my first time to be out on the hill when it was snowing hard all week. Rich and I became powder hounds and wanted to look for new snow to ride on. (Powder is new snow that has just fallen and nobody has skied on it yet.) When you are the first one riding on powder it feels like you are riding on a cloud. We both love it. The best way to find powder is to go way up high into the mountains, and we did. When we went to the top it didn't take long to find what we were looking for. While we were having fun in the powder, we came to a top of a run to take a little rest. When we looked down the hill, we saw that the whole hill was all powder. Rich and I were like, "Wahoo, let's go down!" As we were going down the hill we were doing great until we got in the middle and slowed to a stop and went down. We didn't realize how deep it was. Rich and our skiing buddy were trying to get me out. When they were trying to help, the front of my snowboard went down deeper in the snow, while my tail end went up in the air. All of us were laughing our heads off because we were falling down as we were helping each other out of the snow. We had no idea on how we got in or how we were going to get out of this sticky mess. Rich finally tried pushing down on his handlebar and it made the

board go up and we move a little bit. Rich told me to lean back towards him. It was really hard to do because I was way down deep in the snow, but somehow I managed to get the job done. After about 30 minutes we finally got out of there. I will never forget that awesome powder day.

Every year Snowmass Mountain adds new and fun things to do on the mountain. One year, there was a zip line ride by the Lynn Britt Cabin, one of our favorite places to eat. The zip line ride is where you get strapped into a harness and then you ski down a little hill to pick up enough speed to ride the 10-foot zip line. At the end of it you have to lower yourself down to the ground, because at the end of the zip line it leaves you hanging in the air. I told Rich I wanted to do that.

We went into the tent where you get ready to zip line and we asked one of the workers if a disability kid could go on a zip line. He said, "We never had one before, but let her try and see if she can do the lever that brings you down to the ground after you do the zip line." He then went to get a harness for me and helped me put it on. The harness strapped all around my body for safety. We went to one of the test areas and he clipped me in so I could do the lever. He showed me how it works. He said, "You have to pull the lever towards you and if you pull it down too far it will stop you and you have to push it back up and start again." It was really hard for me to do it. Rich and I decided we would have to come back when we figured everything out. When we got back outside we watched some people go down the zip line to help us get an idea so I could do the zip line.

That afternoon we went to Challenge Aspen to talk to Houston Cowan, the CEO of CA, about me going on the zip line. Houston said, "If Danielle can do it, I want to see it. Let me know if she can do it, and she can do it after the BBQ on Disability Day so everyone can see." Every year on Disability Day, Challenge Aspen has a BBQ at the Lynn Britt Cabin for the staff and all of the ski participants. It was a fun time for me to catch up with my friends. The next day we went back to the tent to try the lever again, and I could do it. Then we had to figure out how to ski down the hill on my own. When we were in the ski school, I saw a saucer sled that gave me an idea that I could ride it down the hill. I told Rich my idea and he liked it. When we knew I could do it, we told Houston.

On the day of the BBQ I was really excited and couldn't wait to go on the zip line. It was also a fun day in the bi-ski, because I was tired of snowboarding and we had to drop off the sled at the Lynn Britt Cabin. Rich put the sled in my arms so he could push me. After we dropped it off, we went off to have fun before lunch. At the BBQ everyone was telling me they couldn't wait to see me on the zip line. That made me really happy inside. When the BBQ was over it was finally time for me to ride the zip line.

While I was putting my harness on all of the Challenge Aspen's staff was lining up with cameras and video cameras because they didn't want to miss the first Challenge Aspen kid who did the zip line. After I got strapped into the zip line, Rich put me into the sled and tied a rope on the sled and around me so it would stay with me when I rode down the hill. After I was all tied up, he asked me if I was ready and I said yes.

Suddenly he gave me a big push to get me going, but my legs fell out and I fell back on the ground and stopped on the hill. We tried again and again but I never got off the ground. After many tries Rich untied the sled and took me out and went to get his skis to be my legs to help me take off into the air. When he got his skis on he picked me up in his arms and we went down the hill while I was still attached to the zip line.

We both yelled, "Holy moly!", because we were scared and couldn't believe what we were doing. We were going really fast. Rich held on to me as long as he could and then let me go. The speed that we were going made me spin like a top all the way down the zip line. When I got down to the end and stopped spinning I was so dizzy, but I did what I needed to do.

I dropped the rope down to the ground to a man who was going to hold it straight

for me while I worked the lever. When I saw the man had the rope I looked back up to start working the lever. Right away I noticed that I had dropped the rope on the side and it was in the way where I was going to pull down the lever, and if I didn't move the rope to the other side I would not be able to get down. I had to think fast.

I yelled down to the man and told him to give me some slack on the rope so I could try to flip the rope over my head to the other side. It was hard to do with the rope already hanging to the ground, but I got it over my head in five minutes. Finally, it was time for the hardest part, pulling the lever.

When I started working on the lever it took me a good five minutes to get it going. When I got it going, I felt like I was going down too fast and I stopped, pulled the lever back up and started again. I did this all the way down to the middle of the rope, and then thought that this was taking forever. Finally I decided to go down with no stopping, and hoped that someone would catch me.

When I went down fast it scared me that I was going to hit the ground hard, but I

stopped where my feet could touch the ground. Rich was right there to hug me, then he raised one of my arms into the air to show everybody that I had made it. I felt really happy that I did the zip line and got down to the ground. Even though I knew it would be hard for me, I still did it.

"Never let your head hang down. Never give up and sit down and grieve. Find another way. And don't pray when it rains if you don't pray when the sun shines." ~

Richard M. Nixon

Here is a story that is scary, funny, or both. I am not going to tell you, you decide.

One year, Rich was out of the ski season for medical reasons. I had to snowboard with a different ski teacher named Spencer and a new buddy. I had to bring them up to speed on how I snowboarded, but they couldn't figure out how to hold the board without my legs hurting on the chairlift. So I decided it would be easier for me to get out of my snowboard and walk to get on and off the chairlift, and it was.

It was also hard to snowboard because it was so hot in March that the snow was melting and I was snowboarding on slush. One day I told Spencer I wanted to go down to Assay Hill to snowboard with my mom and her boyfriend Steve. (My parents were divorced in 2004.) They were learning how to snowboard and I wanted to do some runs with them. We went down to Assay to find them, and I didn't find them until I got in line for the chairlift. I saw Mom in line. We yelled to her and told her what we were doing there, then Steve came sliding in behind us. It was so hot that there was a mud pond with colorful rubber ducks bobbing up and down under the chairlift, and I thought that was funny. I got out of my snowboard to get on to the chairlift.

When it was our turn to get on we did everything as normal. Spencer held my snowboard while the buddy was helping me on. She was so focused on getting me safely on the chairlift that she forgot to lift up her ski tips. Her ski tips got stuck in the mud pond and I saw that she was going down and I felt her arm was still around me and I knew that I was falling with her.

Two clean girls fell five feet in the air into the mud pond. I fell sideways, so the right side of my body was in the mud. The fall really hurt and I started to cry. Steve who was behind us saw what happened and ran over to pull me out of the mud and put me on my back to check me out. I could barely see him because my eyes were all teary and my ski goggles were half covered in mud. The chairlift staff moved us into the locker room, so they can start up the chairlift for the other skiers. In the locker room, Steve checked me out more, and asked me if anything hurt. I told him that my right hip was.

A worker asked if I want to go to the hospital to check out my hip, and I said yes. So the worker called the Ski Patrol to get a snowmobile to take me to the hospital. While the worker was on the phone, Steve called my mom and told her what happened, because she was at the top of the chairlift waiting to snowboard with us. My mom was on the way down to wait with us. We had to wait in the locker room until the Ski Patrol came. While we were waiting, my mom told me to call my dad because I would be with my dad and his girlfriend- Shari. They came out to ski with me, and it was time to spend time with my dad. After I told him what had happened he immediately headed to the hospital to hear what the doctor said.

Ten minutes later a man from the Ski Patrol came and my mom helped me get on the stretcher. She asked me if I wanted to have her ride with me, and I said yes. She got behind me and I got to lean back on her. This was my first time to ride on a Ski Patrol snow mobile. I know most people don't want to be on this ride, never would I, either, but it was my first ride and hopefully my last; it was fun.

When we got to the hospital my mom helped me inside and then my mom told the nurse what had happened to me. After she told the nurse, she showed us to a patient table and gave me big baggy shorts to put on so the doctor could check out my hip x- ray it. I was happy to strip down to my long johns and get out of my muddy ski clothes. While we were waiting for the doctor to come my dad came in. I was happy to see him. Ten minutes later the doctor came in and asked my mom what happened.

The doctor felt my hip, and then took an x -ray to see if anything was broken.

While I was waiting to see the photo of my hip, I was hoping that nothing was broken. I was a little scared, too, because my hip was still hurting from the fall. When the doctor came back with the photo he showed us that nothing was broken. I was really happy about that. He also showed us that I had a little growth gap in my hip and said that I was almost done growing and wouldn't get much taller. I was a little sad about that because I wanted be as tall as my mom. Before we left the doctor gave me a bottle of aspirin to take to help my hip feel better.

After we were done my dad and Shari took me to eat at Brothers Grille with Spencer and my ski buddy. We talked about what happened at the chairlift and talked about me snowboarding the rest of the week. My dad didn't want me to snowboard because he didn't want me to hurt my hip anymore. That night I told my dad that my hip didn't hurt anymore, but he didn't want me to snowboard, and he told me to pack up because we were going back home to Parkville tomorrow. I was so mad that I was not thinking that I could ride the bi-ski the rest of the week.

"Having Cerebral Palsy sometimes I get frustrated but for the most part it is fun to be me."

The next week at school I noticed that I was walking better. My right foot was not rolling in anymore. I told my mom and showed her how I was walking normal. I asked my mom how could it be that I was walking better. She was thinking about my fall at the chairlift and asked me which side I fell on. I told her the right side. Then we realized that my fall somehow loosened my hip and made me walk better. We were amazed that the fall helped me. I was walking like this for a whole month. I was really happy and surprised the fall helped me instead of hurting me.

While I have been snowboarding with Rich, we have been in magazines and made a lot of videos for other people to see what we are doing. One year, when I was in 8th grade, we had a disability week. During that whole week there were a lot of papers on the walls about people with challenges who were in the Special Olympics as well as their quotes. I also knew there was going to be an assembly that was dedicated to the Special

Olympics kids, because the kids were talking about it every day in my Special Ed class. There also going to be a basketball game between the students and the teachers and I couldn't wait to see that.

One day, the principal came up to me and asked me if he could show a video clip of me snowboarding in the assembly on Friday and I said yes! I was so happy that I told my mom and dad right away when I got out of school. Both of them were really excited for me and asked me what time the assembly was so they could come see me, and I told them. I couldn't wait until Friday.

On Friday, during school, the principal called me down to the gym to show me what would happen at the assembly so I would know what to do and what to expect. He told me that the P.E. teacher would say some words about me and then he would call me to come out to stand by him and watch my video.

The principal asked me if that would be fine, and I said yes. I thought it would not be a big deal at the time. Then I went back to my normal school day, and soon enough it was assembly time. I was so excited that everybody would know and see how I snowboarded. When everybody was sitting down for the assembly, my mom and dad came to say hi and good luck to me. I asked my dad to sit with me and he did. I felt really happy about that. Finally, it was time for the assembly to begin.

The P.E. teacher started the show off by welcoming everybody to the "Students vs

Teachers" basketball game. Everybody went wild. Then he said, "Before we get into the game I have some words to say." He went on talking about our Special Olympics athletes and how hard they work. Then he talked about all of the other athletes who are in the

Olympics who have challenges and how they work hard on overcoming their challenges.

Next he said, "We have one of them here right in this school." Then he went on how I

overcame my challenges to become a snowboarder, and then he said, "Come on out

Danielle!" While I got up and got all set in my walker and went to stand by the P.E.

teacher, I heard everybody was whooping and clapping really hard for me. When I heard the crowd cheering for me I felt really happy and then I got butterflies in my stomach.

When I got to the middle of the gym where the P.E. teacher was, he asked me a question, then he put the microphone up to my face so everybody could hear my answer. When he put it up it up to my mouth, I felt my nerves go crazy, my face got really hot, and I hoped my face wasn't getting redder and redder so no one could see that I was nervous. It took me about five seconds to spit out my answer. After I answered he told everyone about the video and then he hit play.

When the video began I felt calmer. The video was when Rich and I went into the Little Makaha Park to get some big air. When I saw Rich and me getting big air going off of each jump I was amazed on how high we got. Then I saw myself going on a rail and I remember how Rich talked me into it and I was scared. I didn't want to do it, but I did it and was so proud of myself. I also remember at the end of the day my legs were like noodles and I could barely walk because I wanted to go big and go sky high for the video.

My model is to go big or go home, and I always want and try to go big.

When the video was over everybody went wild and the P.E. teacher said thank you. On the way back to my seat I was thinking that this was so cool on how I showed my whole middle school in Parkville what I do in Snowmass.

During my snowboarding years Rich and I tried a lot of different models of rider bars. This included adding to the original PVC handlebar, the seat, and Rich's handlebar. The Freedom Factory ultimately crafted their version of handlebars, which we added to, again. These were made out of aluminum and were adjustable, but proved too shaky and had too much play in the bar. The issue was that the handlebars just needed to be better attached. If we go riding our hardest in the half pipe, or anywhere else, we bent the handle or the bar and it would make us fall, or we had to stop and pound the bar back into shape.

It was really dangerous and we had to take our time to make it down the mountain in one piece each and every day. Rich's handlebars were solid and more stable then the adjustable version. We realized we needed a better design and attachment for the handlebars. In early 2011 Rich called his brother, Arthur Ganson, to ask him if he could make a steadier snowboard for me, and he said yes. Arthur is an amazing engineer.

He is a famous kinetic artist, just Google his name and you will know what I am talking about. He and Rich worked together to make a high tech machine snowboard for me. It took a long time to build, but finally, in March 2012 I got to ride it. The new handlebars are aluminum and too soft. It's a bit too heavy and not still enough, but that is all we could do for this next version until we knew all was right and we would need more money for the expensive material - titanium. On each side there are shocks that will hold our hardest jumps.

Finally, for my harness and my legs, they made the bar so I can lean back in the harness and recline when my legs are tired. The harness holds me in a more neutral place while resting which the old strap and pad could never do. This is key!

Oh, I almost forgot two important parts. The first thing is that they made the bar farther away from my body, so I can go into my toe turn without the bar stopping me.

(With the old snowboard, the bar was right against my stomach so I couldn't go into my toe turn as far as I needed to.) The second thing is that we bought two GoPro cameras we can attach anywhere on the snowboard and even on our helmets to make our own snowboard movies. This was a very fun part of my life growing up.

When the day came for me to ride my new snowboard for the first time I was so excited and couldn't wait to rip down the hill. First, I had to go to Challenge Aspen's equipment room to get everything fit just right for me. After about two hours it was time to do my first run on my new high tech snowboard.

When we got to the hill, I got strapped in and ready to go. I felt like the happiest kid on earth, because I was about to take a new, smooth snowboard for the ride of my life. (Oops, I meant young adult because I was 20 at that time, but you know what I mean.) I feel like a kid still today.

After Rich helped me in, he had to get into his skis. He got into the first ski just fine, but with the second one he couldn't get his boot to snap into to his ski. He kept on kicking his boot and trying to snap into his ski, but after about the 100th time he realized that his binding was broken. We both broke out into a fit of laugher because we were almost on our first ride on our dream machine that we dreamt of for two years, and we had to wait another five minutes for Rich to get his long skis.

What are the odds? Finally, when Rich got into his long skis we were ready to go. When we were going down the hill we both could feel a huge difference, the ride was as smooth as butter. It was amazing.

During that week we tried a lot of different ways to make the snowboard better and we did.

The next year, in 2013, Rich wanted me to make every move on my own, like I was the driver and he was just along for the ride, and there if I needed help. By the end of the week I was making my own turns and was in control of my own speed. Rich was barely holding on. I was really happy about that. I also did my first hockey stop. It was just a little one, but my goal is to get better at that so I can spray snow up into Rich's face. On the last day we decided to weave through the trees just like old times.

We were having a blast until we fell into a hole that we didn't see. Somehow the front nose of my snowboard got stuck in the hole and it made me go up sideways, like I was walking on a building like Spiderman. Then lucky enough, I fell on my back. Rich was behind me and tried to jump over the snowboard rig and me so he didn't land on top

of me, but he landed on top of the bar and his ski boot hit my neck.

You would think that I would start to cry because a hard boot hitting my neck would hurt, and it did, but I went into an insane laugher. We all started to laugh. The best part of all was one of the GoPro cameras that was on the snowboard was in the right spot where it was looking right on my face and got my laughing face on that fall. That night when we got home we started to download all of the videos to my laptop from that week.

It took the whole night so I couldn't watch the videos until the next day.

The next morning, when I woke up, I went straight to my laptop to look for the falling video. When I found the video, I watch it over and over because; I was amazed and laughing at the same time. The video looked like Rich's boot was going to chop my head right off! I am happy that I didn't lose my head, but if I did, I probably would become the headless snowboarder and snowboard the mountains all the time and scare my Challenge Aspen friends. (You can watch that fall in one of my snowboard videos I made and a lot more at www.dancanshred.com. I will tell you about my website and how

I make my snowboard videos later in this book.)

Since I became the first adaptive snowboarder in 2001, I have had fun being the

Guinea pig and helping build the snowboard better than ever. I have given permission to CA to let the Wounded Warriors, who are disabled Veterans, use my snowboard. So far, Rich has only used it with a paraplegic who has been in a wheelchair for 25 years. I hope one day we can build more snowboards like mine and let other people with disabilities who want to snowboard have a chance to do it. I want them to feel like a free bird and feel the wind in their faces just like

Snowmass Angel the Biography of Danielle Coulter

CHAPTER FOUR

Growing Up in a Musical Family, and Making it into a Passion

"In every conceivable manner, the family is link to our past, bridge to our future." ~ Alex Haley

Since I was born, I realized that everyone in my family has a musical gene inside of them, and every house has a piano in it. Everyone could play an instrument or sing a tune. When my mom took me to see Dr. Chopra, he said the best thing for me to do was to listen to classical music. He said he thought that it would help me think better, and suggested to get some kid's instruments so I could make my own music. When we got home, my mom went out to buy a lot of instruments and CDs for me. I love to listen and make music on my own. It makes my whole body happy to hear music.

Every time I go over to my aunt's house I always go to the music basket to get something to make noise with, and even my cousins get in on the fun. We play music together for hours. Sometime we have to be as quiet as a mouse, because my uncle records in his recording studio down in the basement for his Irish rock band, "The Elders". That is no fun to us. When we got older our parents signed us up for piano lessons with the same teacher. We went to the teacher's house once a week. It was hard and took a long time for me to learn how play the songs. I couldn't understand how to read the music sheets and my hands were too shaky to hit the right key at the same time. I got really frustrated, but I didn't give up.

One day, my piano teacher decided I could compose my own song with the use of an orange in my hand for my first piano recital. She decided that an orange would be perfect for me to hold in my hand to hit keys with, because it was big to hold and it was hard for me to hit the right keys with my hands. I practiced and practiced every week with my teacher on my orange song. It was pretty cool that I could put sounds together with my ears but not be able to read notes on a music sheet.

I was like Beethoven on deciding what to put in my masterpiece. I told my teacher what keys to play and she would play them. Remember the saying, "My right hand man?" Well, she was my right hand woman, because I had to hold myself upright on the piano bench. I couldn't play with both of my hands, because if I did I would have fallen right off of the bench. So she was my other hand, and she had an orange, too.

I worked so hard to make my orange song, and when it was almost recital day I had come up with the coolest orange song. When I played it at recital I felt really happy and proud that I played a song I composed myself. Years later I even did a duet with my cousin Zac at Park University, which is where I went to school for two years.

I love to hang out with my family and play music whenever I can. That's why back in Chapter Two I said yes to go to Challenge Aspen's Magic of Music and Dance Camp. Like when I couldn't wait for my first day of skiing, I felt the same way about this camp. When the first day finally came, I woke up with a huge smile and couldn't wait to meet and make new friends.

The camp was held at the Aspen Club where I did Pilates for that summer. I thought that was pretty cool because I was already familiar with the building. When I got there my mom showed me into a room with a lot of people with a lot of abilities and disabilities. Some had CP like me, like my friends Win, Rochelle, and Max who I met at the camp. We are still good friends up to this day. I even saw my ski teacher Rich and he was into music, too. He was my buddy that week, and I was really happy about that.

When it was time to start camp everybody got into a huge circle to talk about the week and introduce ourselves. We had to tell everybody our buddy's name and what he or she liked to do. It was a fun way to meet everybody. Then the director, Cathy Crum, told us what play we were going to perform on Friday. The play was called "The Messing Room", it was a spoof off of Peter Pan. It was a lot of fun putting it together.

During the week we rehearsed in the mornings, and then in the afternoons we went down to the gym, the ball pit room, or even go out on the town to do outdoor activities to let everyone relax from the play, and get to know one another. In the mornings, sometimes we had a dance out time, where you can dance any way you wanted.

I always loved that time because everyone got crazy. I tried my best at dancing in my walker. I watched how everybody danced with their arms, and their whole body, but all that I could do was shake my hips back and forth. Then I saw Cathy dancing like crazy with her whole body. That day I realized that I wanted to work on getting out of my walker and be like everyone else because I could do so little in my walker.

The rest of the week was a blast getting ready for the show, and being around my new lifelong friends. At the end of the week we had put on a great show, and it was hard to say good-bye, but I knew that I would see them next year.

When I go home I always think of my friends, the great times we had, and always had the determination of getting out of my walker and walking on my own. I had so much fun that I couldn't wait to go back next year. The next year when I got the play camp papers in the mail and heard the play was "When You Wish upon a Star", a Disney

Medley", I asked my cousin, AnnaLea, if she would like to come and be my buddy, because I knew she would love it. She said, "Yes!" When we got there she fit right in and met everybody. (When we get together at camp we feel like a crazy acting family.) This year everybody got to decide which Disney character they wanted to be. I chose to be

Mulan. AnnaLea was my grandmother and we wanted to dance to the song "Reflection" from the movie. AnnaLea made up the moves for us to dance, and Rochelle sang the song as a cute Mini-Mouse.

At that time it was the first year I had my leg braces on and they helped me stand up better. This meant I could lean back on my walker a little bit and do the dance moves with my hands, and I was really happy about that. We had fun doing that act and the show.

After the show my mom came up to me and said, "I didn't recognize you with all of your make-up and that black wig on". "Come on let take that wig off." She grabbed my shoulders and tried to take of the wig. I yelled, "Mom, that is my real hair! They dyed it for the show." My mom was so mad that when we got home she made me wash the dye out right away. I guess it just didn't look right.

During the whole year off of play camp, I told my mom to hold me by my hips when I walked, because I had my leg braces on and I didn't want to use my walker. (My mom has been holding me on her hip for far too long, and now I wanted her to hold my hips.)

On Mother's Day of 2000, my family and I went to Paradise Grill, a restaurant that used to be in Parkville, to celebrate. When we get together on a holiday I always love hanging out with everyone. This Mother's Day wasn't a normal one. At some point I told my mom that I had to use the powder room. My mom helped me down out of my seat and held my hips as we walked to the powder room. We had to turn two corners to get to the long hallway to get to the powder room. When we were walking down the long hallway I said, "Mom, let go of me." I had to tell her that three times before she took her hands off of my hips. When she did, I took my first steps all by myself. I knew that I had made my mom very proud that day. I just knew it was time for her to let go and I walked.

That summer at play camp everyone was surprised to see me walking on my own without my walker on the first day of camp. I was holding my arms out to keep my balance and I fell a lot, but I didn't care, I was walking on my own. When I fall, I just get back up and keep on going like the "Energizer Bunny." The play that we were going to put on was "The Wizard of Oz". I got the part of Glinda the Good Witch, and Cathy wanted me to walk down the yellow brick road with all of my friends who were the yellow brick road walkers because she wanted to show everybody how I walked.

I was really excited and couldn't wait until show day. I practiced and practiced walking down the yellow brick road every day until the big show day. (Oh yeah, I even practiced my lines and the songs, if I didn't there would be a dead spot, and we don't want that now do we?)

When the big day came, I was so excited that I couldn't even bear it. When the show began I was on the sideline all in black with AnnaLea, and our friend, Bo. (I forgot to tell you that I was a part of the tornado, too.) When it was time for the tornado scene we came out and spun around like crazy. When we were done I was so dizzy. We got off stage and I had to rip off my black cloak, revealing my pink Glinda dress, and get ready for the next scene. Now let me tell you when you have CP, walking and being dizzy don't mix. Lucky for me, I had a couple of minutes to pull myself together before I went out again to welcome Dorothy to Munchkin Land. When the scene was done, the next scene I was in was where I was going to walk down the yellow brick road.

I was on the sidelines watching my friends dance to the song "Ease on Down the

Road." As I watched, I was listening to the words of the song.

"Come on

Ease on down, Ease on down the road (ease on down) Come on

Ease on down, Ease on down the road (ease on down)

Don't you carry nothing that might be a load

Come on

Ease on down, Ease on down, down the road"

As I was listening to the song, I told myself to ease on down the road. When it was about time for me to ease on down the road my friend Leah's mom came and pulled me off the wall, because I didn't have good enough balance to stand on my own back then. I had to lean on something to stand up. I was like a fly on a wall.

Leah's mom took me by my hips and lined me up with the yellow brick road so I was ready to go when Cathy yelled out my name. When Cathy did, I took off. When I was walking I could feel the joy busting out of me, because I wanted to walk all by myself since the first year of camp, and now, I was on stage doing it. I could hear all of my friends whooping and hollering, and that made me even more joyful.

At the other end of the road I saw Bo and Liz there ready to catch me. I was so close to them, and then about two feet away I fell and rolled to them like a big bowling pin. They helped me back up and sent me back the way I came. I saw Leah's mom's arms were open to catch me. When I got into her arms we did a huge bear hug and spun around. At that moment, I felt like the happiest camper that met her goal, and I knew it was only the beginning of my walking journey, and it wasn't going to end here. I wasn't going to see my end of the yellow brick road for a long time.

Over the years our acting family's bond grew stronger and stronger. We love to help each other out, joke around, have paint wars when we are painting the sets, and sometime pull pranks on each other. My favorite thing of all coming back to camp is to see my old friends and make new friends, because we get new campers every year. One year when we did "The Little Mermaid", I was a mermaid sister and the seahorse announcer.

On Friday during our last dress rehearsal I was watching the scene where Chef Louie is chasing Sebastian around the kitchen. Remember how this scene goes in the movie? Well, when Cathy is in charge, everyone knows that she will put her own spin on it and make it even funnier. She asked Robert and his buddy to come running out with big carrot stuffed toys in hand and even Amy who was playing the dog to help Sebastian get away from Chef Louie.

It looked like so much fun that I wanted to join in. After the rehearsal I asked

Cathy and she said, "Yes!" When we were going through the scene Robert and his buddy came up. Robert's buddy told Cathy that Robert was too scared and didn't want to do the scene. So I was stepping into Robert's place and helped out, too. I love when I help my friends out. When I got back into the makeup room I told my friends what was going on. When Dan (Dan the Man) heard it, he gave me a hard time like always. He said, "With your tight mermaid dress on, it will be hard to run in. You will fall into the pot and become fried fish." I talked back to him with a lot of no's and I wanted to prove him wrong.

During the real show, before Robert's buddy and I went running on stage with our big carrots, I was thinking of taking little baby running steps so I wouldn't fall. When I heard the old time chasing music come on, I bolted out of the wings. About two seconds in I fell flat on my butt. Lucky enough, I fell behind the dinner table where Ariel, Eric, and his family were waiting on their food which was running away, so no one who was watching the play saw my fall.

I turned my head over my shoulder and mouthed, "Help!" One of the buddies came running and helped me get back on my feet, and I took off again. I was in my crazy and worry state all at the same time. Because a lot of my friends were running around, we wanted to make this scene as funny as we could, and I didn't want to fall again where everybody could see me. I had a lot to think about. At some point I almost ran into the man who was playing Chef Louie.

I'm happy that I didn't fall on him, because if I did I would probably have bounced off of him and flown into the pot: making me a flying fish that just got fried. After that play, I felt really happy that I helped by stepping in for a friend plus, I had a wild and crazy time.

Sometimes when we are working so hard on the play to get it ready in time for Friday, we add stuff in the day before the show. That sounds impossible to do but we get it done. And other times when we have everything nailed down the day before, and on Friday almost every year something goes wrong we always have to improvise and go with the flow. One year we were putting on "Peter Pan". I was Tinker Bell and during the week I had to run around to a lot of scenes to practice, plus, I had to work with my friend Guewny, who has autism. I had to help her move around the stage and danced with her. She was Tinker Bell Two; she was like my little fairy sister, and I loved that and loved helping her. A lot was going on.

On Thursday, we get all the pieces of the play together and everybody gets to see each other's hard work, which I love. Everything was going fine until the scene where I had to drink Peter Pan's medicine that was poisoned by Captain Hook. After I came back to life by the love of clapping, Cathy asked me if I could get back up on my feet from the floor on my own, and I said no.

Then she came up with a crazy idea where my friend Jeff who was Peter Pan would help me up. Jeff and I were speechless; because we were thinking that there was no way we could pull this off. I was twice as tall as Jeff, and he himself was pretty shaky on his feet. There was no way that he could help me up.

Cathy kept encouraging us that we could do it, and she was right by our sides, working with us. We kept working on it until we got it, and when we got it, all of us were excited that we finally did it. The next day was the big show day. When we did our last rehearsal everything went really well, but during the real show it went downhill.

After everybody helped me come back to life, I got up on my knees and got ready for Jeff to help me up. Before he helped me, he ran off to the other side of the stage and said his last line. I guess he forgot to help me and was in a hurry to say his line. Everybody in the wings including me yelled to him to help me up. Jeff came back to help me. Everybody in the house and backstage went wild. While we were getting ready to do our thing, Julie, our pianist, was playing a tune to make the scene more fun. When Jeff and I were ready to go I started to pull up.

I got to my feet, Jeff let go of me and I fell down. Everybody yelled, "Oh!", but I got back up on my knees and got ready again. Everybody was yelling and clapping for us. They were also nervous for us, especially Julie, because she was playing the piano faster and faster. When I was on my feet again, Jeff asked, "Are you good?" I said, "Yes", but when he let go I fell down again. I got back into the ready position again. We both were laughing way too hard that we couldn't pull it off. We looked into the wings for help. Jeff's buddy came running out to save the day. When I got up everyone went crazy. After that show when I got all the laughter out of me, I was happy that I didn't give up and kept

on trying.

I have one more story to tell you that goes with my Tinker Bell fall. The next summer when I was at Challenge Aspen's art camp, we went horseback riding at T-Lazy7 Ranch one afternoon. There were a lot of campers so we had to split into two groups and do two rounds of horseback riding. I stayed back and waited to go on the second round. When I was hanging around with my friends we got bored. When we were driving in I had seen an old playground set. I told Bo and Zac I want to go swing.

They were both in so we started walking over there. While we were walking Gweny and her buddy decided to join us, and were right behind us. When we got there we thought the swing set was over 50 years old. Gweny and I got on the two swings side by side and started to swing. Gweny's buddy said, "The two Tinker Bells are flying again!" It was a lot of fun swinging with Gweny, but soon I was swinging sideways. Bo asked if I wanted to get off and I said no. Back then I was only thinking about fun and not being safe, because I was 13 and liked to be daring. Over time my swing became more like a bucking bronco, and it kicked me off. I fell flat on my back hitting the ground.

When I opened my eyes everybody asked if I was okay and we all started to laugh. I said,

"Yeah, yeah, I'm okay. What's happened?" My friend Doug said, "You did a cartwheel five feet in the air, and I wish I had a video camera to tape that!" We laughed some more, and I am happy I didn't get hurt.

I love coming back to Magic of Music and Dance Camp every year to see my

friends and put a great show on. Now that I am older it amazes me how we pull a show off in one week from auditions on Monday to an outstanding show on Friday. To you this sounds impossible, but we get it done.

CHAPTER FIVE

Finding My Own Instrument

"Because of her singing they all went away feeling moved, feeling comforted, feeling, perhaps, the slightest tremors of faith." ~ Ann Patchett

When I was growing up in my musical family, I was trying my best to fit in. Every time we had family music time my aunt gave me every instrument you could shake, while the rest of my family played string instruments. When I was older I wanted to play guitar and piano just like my cousins. My cousins tried to help me; they didn't treat me any different, as if I didn't have CP, and I like that. I tried to play guitar and piano like my cousins for years, but I couldn't get it.

One year when I was skiing in Snowmass Rich invited me to one of his music gigs at a restaurant right by Snowmass Mountain called The Cirque. (The Cirque is now called Venga Venga.) It was fun watching Rich play his guitar in his friends' band. The guy that was playing the drums was Billy Joel's drummer.

He was really good. Rich decided to give me a little taste on how Billy Joel's drummer played. After a while Rich announced who I was and invited me to come up and play drums with Billy Joel's drummer. I was blown away and before I knew it I was on his lap in front of his rock 'n roll drum set. Before the band started to play the next song Billy Joel's drummer gave me his drumsticks. I had no idea what was about to happen because I didn't know how to play the drums.

Then the band started to play. Within seconds Billy Joel's drummer grabbed my hands and off we went. I was amazed watching his and my hands dancing all around the drum set. Our hands were going like 20 miles per hour. I was having the best time of my life. After that day Rich and I knew it was the start of my drumming days. Over the years I played bongo and sang with Rich at gigs, played outside of the Lynn Britt Cabin on Snowmass Mountain, and even played at the yearly ski party for all of the ski instructors for the Aspen Ski Company. It was a blast!

When I was in fifth grade all of my friends tried out for the fifth grade choir. For the first half of the school year I watched them perform whenever I got the chance. It was a lot of fun seeing my friends singing and I wished I had tried out. By the end of the school year we got out for the holidays. Our music teacher made an announcement to the fifth grade that if you wanted to sign up for the choir after the holidays you could. I was so excited that I could hardly believe it, and couldn't wait to sign up.

On the first day back to school I went to the music room and signed up for choir. When I got in it was a lot of fun singing with my friends. We sang all over Kansas City. My favorite place we sang at was at the Kansas City Wizards soccer game. We sang the national anthem on their home field. It was pretty awesome to be on the field singing to hundreds of people. I loved every moment of singing in the choir and decided to continue on with the sixth grade choir.

Some of my friends stayed in choir with me but I also made some new ones. One of my sixth grade aids, Miss Groves, came with me to choir to help me out. She loved to sing and sang outside of school to make more money. Also, her daughter, Tayla, was in choir, too because she had her mother's musical gene like I did with my family. I had fun singing with them. My favorite place to sing that year was at the event "Christmas on The River". "Christmas on The River" is a Parkville, Missouri event that celebrates Christmas on the first Friday in December. It is a huge event that happens in the heart of downtown Parkville by the Missouri River. There is a lot to do: shows, eating food, seeing the big man himself, and petting his reindeer. If you name anything that reminds you about Christmas I bet it would be there.

Every year choirs from all of the schools in the Park Hill District come together and sing Christmas songs on the big stage. I was happy to be one of those kids. I had fun singing with my friends. Miss Groves and Tayla were standing right by me. When we were singing "Rudolph the Red Nose Reindeer", Tayla and I broke the rules and sang/yelled all the fun in-between lines. I don't know who made the rule that we couldn't sing the fun lines, but we did it anyway. I had a blast and will never forget that year when I was hanging out and singing with Tayla and her mom.

When I got out of sixth grade for the summer, I started thinking of the Magic of

Music and Dance Camp, like every summer, but this summer wasn't going to be normal.

When I got to camp I saw we had more kids than ever before, and our play was "Snow

White and the Seven Dwarfs". We had so many kids that Cathy decided to turn the word

"Seven" into "Seventeen" so we would have parts for every kid. I thought this would be the funniest play we had ever done.

On the first day, we were holding auditions. Cathy asked, "Who wants to try out for a singing solo?" The room was silent. At that moment I had a thoughts running through my mind. Should I go for it? Then I thought if Tayla and her mom could sing I could do it, too. Then I broke the silence with two words, "I do!" Everybody was shocked that I was the one who spoke up. I got up and stood by the piano with Julie. Cathy gave me the lyrics to the song "A Smile and a Song" and I started to sing. While I was singing Julie played the piano slow so the tune could match up with my singing. At that time I couldn't sing at the normal tempo. I sang as best as I could. When I finished everyone went crazy. Cathy was amazed and told me good job. I was happy that I took the chance and followed my gut.

During that week I practiced my lines and solo. By Friday I was ready to go, and after the show everybody told me that I did a great job and I made them cry. I asked my mom, "Could you understand me?" She said, "Yes, every word." I felt really happy about that. Then I was thinking about how I talked.

When I talk to people I have no idea why they can't understand me because when I talk I can hear my voice as normal, like an able-bodied person. When people hear me talk they can hear my CP talk, which I can't hear. I realized when I practiced my lines and solo for a long time I could be understood. I don't know how it works, but it does. I

finally found my own instrument, my voice.

Over the years I worked really hard on singing better with singing solos at camp.

One year we put on the play "Annie". In June, I got the soundtrack and practiced daily on singing the song "Tomorrow." I practiced singing with the song playing in the background and in the mirror. One day, I realized I wanted to hear my voice as other people hear me, but how do I do that? The answer and the tool was right on my Mac laptop. I opened up Photo Booth and turned on video mode and recorded myself singing. After I finished, I played the video and that really helped me hear what I sounded like to other people. I repeated this task millions of times to get ready for play camp.

On the first day of play camp we were holding auditions. I always have the normal reaction of having a case of the nerves. Am I really going to do this? When it was time to try out for "Annie" and sing "Tomorrow" I went right on up. As my friends were singing one by one I could feel my nerve build up. When it was time for me to sing I was able to sing.

When I was singing my nerves somehow went away. When I finished my song, everybody went crazy and I felt a big relief and felt really happy that I did it. I hoped that

I would get to sing "Tomorrow." When it was time to announce the cast, I got excited. There were five kids who were casted as Annie because we had so many kids; I was one of them, and I got the part of the Annie who got to sing "Tomorrow." My friend Max who has CP also, got the part of Sandy the dog.

I was really happy that I was singing to him. Max was born was an able-bodied person, but at the age of three, he choked on a popcorn kernel and got a kind of CP where he can't move very well and lost his voice. This year when we rehearsed, everybody was amazed that when I sang it made Max really happy and he moved his arms for the first time. When I saw that I felt joy running through my body because I was surprised my singing could be so powerful that it made my friend's arms move. It also made everybody cry that year. I don't mean to make them cry, but I do. I had a blast singing to Max, and I was happy that I sang the whole song by myself for the first time.

Do you know when a play critic comes to see you in a play and you are so nervous? Well, what if you didn't know who was watching the play and who they were? One year we preformed the play "Grease". I was Sandy who sang "Hopelessly Devoted to You." The night after the play my family and I had Rich over for dinner and just hung out after a hectic week. Rich told me he had big news to tell me and wanted my approval before telling anybody else.

He said, "Houston told me a lady who is the Director of the Challenge Aspen's Vince Gill and Amy Grant Golf Classic fundraiser event told him she wants you to sing at the event. Do you want to do that?" (Houston Cowan is the CEO of Challenge Aspen.) I said yes right away. The night of the event there were a lot of stars there besides Vince and Amy. Before they came up and did their show Rich and I went up on stage with our guitar and drum and sang, "You've Got a Friend" by James Taylor. We sang this song because we had been friends for so long and it says everything.

It was so awesome to be there to sing to 700 people. At the end of the show Amy called everyone who sang that night including us to come back on stage and sing

"You've Got a Friend" again. Somehow, I ended up leaning up against and holding hands with Vince. When I was singing with everybody I felt 100 percent amazing to be singing with singers who are known all over the USA. It was one of the best nights of my life.

Through the years acting has become a passion for me. When I act and sing I feel that CP drain out of my body and I am in the moment. I love to be someone else for a while and walk in their shoes. I would love to act and sing more than one time a year. When I was in middle school I tried out for the play every year. I had no idea what to expect.

The first year play was "Honk". "Honk" is the story about the Ugly Duckling. At the meeting before the try-out the choir teacher, Mr. Belloff, who put on the play, told us what to expect. I didn't think it would take two months to get the play ready. That's longer then my play camp but I didn't care. He handed us papers to get ready for the tryouts. When I got home I practiced the slowest song in the play because I sing my best when the song is slow.

At the tryouts, I sang the best that I could and I got in as part of the ensemble. I had no idea what an ensemble was, but soon I learned that it is a group of singers that help tell the story through song. I thought that was going to be easy because I love singing, but I sure was wrong.

As days went by, we were busy reading and singing the play in the classroom, it was then time to work on stage. For the first time in my life I had to learn how to dance like everybody else in my walker. Mr. Belloff gave me plain B moves but I wanted to dance just like my friends. I worked really hard to do so. When it was time to talk about costumes Mr. Belloff told all of us who were a part of the ensemble that we needed three costumes: a bird, a frog, and a bed sheet, to be a snow person.

In my head, I was like, "What? I can't quick change", but then I thought of it like a challenge and I was determined to do it. When I got home I looked through my closet and put all of my costumes together. They were all pull-on because I couldn't do ties, buttoning, and zippers. (Still to this day I can't do them.) The last two weeks of rehearsal was dress rehearsal. Every night I worked my butt off to get everything down.

The order of the play for me was to be a blue bird in my first two scenes, a frog next, then a snow person, and in the last scene back into a blue bird. The play run time was one hour and fifteen minutes with no black outs or intermission. With that in mind, I was on high alert to get this play down under my belt and be like my able-bodied friends.

During the dress rehearsal, I was running around backstage like a chicken with his head cut off. I was in and out of the dressing room, had layers of costumes on, and happy to have a little down time. I was glad I could quick change 95% on my own and I had to ask my friends to help me with the other 5%. On stage was another fun story. With my first year of dancing in my walker I kept up with everybody. My favorite scene was when my friends and I were frogs and singing and dancing to the song "Warts and All." By opening night I had everything down and rocked it. The next year the play was "Aladdin" and it had way more dancing then "Honk". I was happy to pull those two plays off and learn how to dance in my walker just like my able-bodied friends.

Once I got into high school I worked hard to be a part of acting in some way. I got into the theater club and tried out for every play. When I didn't get a part in the play I always asked my acting teacher, Miss Whitt, if I could help with the play in some way.

She said yes and gave me the job of passing the playbills to the people.

I was really happy that I helped even though I didn't get a part in the play. I tried out every year and when I was a senior I got a part of a daughter in the play "Fiddler on the Roof." I was so happy that I finally got in and acted with my acting friends one more time before we graduated from high school. I really had fun acting with my acting friends that I acted with in middle school. I will never forget my Park Hill South High School acting family.

Every year in May our theater club has an end of the year celebration with a play, acts, awards, and the most important part - food. At our last meeting of the school year my friend, Kaelyn, who was the president of the Acting Club, was talking about the end of the year celebration night. The top subject was the awards ceremony. Before Miss Whitt gives out the awards the officers usually talk about the parts of acting and perform them: dancing, acting, and singing. This year was different.

Kaelyn opened it up to everybody to act, sing, or dance. She said, "If you want to perform, come talk to me or one of the other officers after the meeting." I thought that this was the perfect time to show my friends how I could sing. For the past few years when I tried out for plays in school I sang at the normal speed of a song. (I tried my best.) I wanted to show my friends how I sing my best, by singing at my speed, slow.

After the meeting I went up to Kealyn and asked if I could sing. When I asked

Kealyn she said, "Yes, what song do you want to sing?" I told her I wanted to sing "This is Me" and she put me down on the list. The song "This is Me" is from the Disney movie Camp Rock. It is about when you come out of the dark and show people who you really are. I picked it out because I sang it in one of our Challenge Aspen's play and the story is a lot like me. (But that is not the case now because you are reading my life story.)

That night when I got home I realized I couldn't sing my best with normal speed of the song on the CD, and I needed to figure out a way to slow down the song. I opened up the app, Garage Band, to see what I could do. I dropped the song into the working space and just played around.

After a while I found what I was looking for, the controls for the speed. I could make the song speed up or slow down; in this case I wanted it to slow down. It took some time to find the right tempo to go with my singing, but I finally found it. Every night I practiced and practiced to get ready for the big night. The night before the celebration I

came down with a bad cold and a frog in my throat.

Now you are thinking I would back down, no way Jose! I go by the actors' saying, "The show must go on." I had been sick when I was dancing around the stage in

"Aladdin", but it wasn't as bad as this. I stayed low that night and the next day at school. I drank a lot of hot tea and took throat drops. That night at the celebration I took what I could from the house to help my voice and used them before I went on.

When the celebration began I was so nervous, but I had to stick to the plan. My friends were counting on me. I was thinking why am I the one who gets sick the night before I sing? but you have got to deal with what you have at the time. When I heard my name I went up on stage and sang the best that I could. After I was done everyone went crazy and were crying. Like I said before I don't mean to make people cry. I was so happy that I pulled that off even though I was sick. By the end of the night I got two awards plus being named Thespian of the year. I also got a Minnie Mouse voice but I didn't care.

Miss Witt presented the award to me, but before she announced the recipient of Thespian of the year, she explained how she came to her decision. She said there were many excellent actors. She looked up the criteria of a Thespian, and besides earning all the points, stars, and lettering in Drama, she said one person had tried out consistently for every play and even though they didn't always get a part they remained in high spirits and asked what they could do to help. This person embodied the spirit of what it was to be a Thespian. Miss Witt then announced the Thespian of the year award goes to

Danielle Coulter.

In the past 16 years of doing the Magic of Music and Dance Camp I was getting better at acting, singing, dancing, and learning the ropes. In 2009, Cathy asked Win, Rochelle, and me to come on board to be on the Challenge Aspen play staff and become director's assistants. Cathy picked all three of us because we were at the first camp and because she saw that we were capable of helping others. We were so excited! Cathy told us that we were going to do a sequel to "The Broadway Café". "The Broadway Café" was written by Cathy and Tom Paxton. (Tom always helps out and plays the biggest parts in the plays. Mostly the villains, and he always makes me laugh, especially when he plays

a girl.)

"The Broadway Café" is based off of plays we have done in the past, like "Peter Pan", "Grease", and many more. The story line is an owner named Joe who opens a new café called Joe's Café. (Now I know what you are thinking that we based the play off of the Broadway's play "Joe's Café", but we didn't.) Joe hired a chef named Nelly who loves to sing and dance, but Joe doesn't like it. At the beginning of the play Joe's café is empty until Nelly turns Joe's Café into The Broadway Café with a lot of musical acts. During the show, Joe doesn't like what Nelly was doing to the café and it becomes chaotic, but in the end, Joe loves what Nelly has done to the café.

When Win, Rochelle, and I heard what we were doing we shot ideas out in emails back and forth between Cathy and us like ping-pong balls all year long. Win, Rochelle, and I all have CP and when we get on something so exciting like this it is really hard to stop. In May, everybody got together for a meeting at Cathy's house. Everybody lives in Colorado except for me. At that time I was finishing up my school year in Parkville and I couldn't be at the meeting in person, but I wished I could.

Win brought her laptop so I could be there by video cam. Win Kelly Charles is my lifetime best friend to this very day. It was a lot of fun seeing everyone and it was better than being on a phone. Before the meeting Cathy offered me juice and a muffin and put them in front of Win's laptop and we all laughed. During the meeting we shared ideas and learned what it takes to make the camp come together before the first day of play camp.

It was cool to learn what happens backstage. We talked about the kids who were coming to play camp and which part they would be best at, costumes, props, and the story line of "The Broadway Café II". It was fun shouting ideas back and forth, and lucky for me when I can't be understood I could type what I wanted to say underneath the video cam and hit send to pop up on Win's laptop. At the end of the meeting we came up with a good story line with different themes from around the world for the play. By June we all had our copy of the play, "The Broadway Café II: Around the World." Win, Rochelle, and I got our parts early so we could learn all of our lines and help the other kids at camp.

At the first day of camp we got to watch all the kids audition and then when they were over and everybody went out of the room, Win, Rochelle, and I got to stay and help with the casting. It was a lot of fun but hard work to find a part that fit for everybody and their disability, but we got it done. During the week we were really busy running around helping the kids, directing scenes, and practicing our own scenes.

I didn't have time to sit down and relax with my friends until we did the afternoon activities. We have been on the staff for four years now and it is a lot of work putting a one-hour play together in one week. Sometimes we are over our heads and running around like a chicken with its head cut off, but we love to help the kids. Being around people that we grew up with, and being a part of the staff is pretty special.

I love going to the camp every year to act and be with my acting family and now helping everybody. I went to the first camp in 1998 and have been at the camp for all 16 years and never missed one. Once in one of my acting classes in high school Miss Whitt asked everybody, "How did you get into acting?" The first thing that popped into my mind was the first year of Magic of Music and Dance Camp where I made friendships that would last a life time, good energy that fills up the room with joy and laugher. I love to act anytime and anywhere I can; but, there is no place where I have the same feeling I do as when I am at this play camp.

When you have passion for something you love to do, stick with it and don't let other people tell you what you can and cannot do.

Snowmass Angel the Biography of Danielle Coulter

CHAPTER SIX

The Making of Dan Can Shred

"These days the technology can solve our problems and then some. Solutions may not only erase physical or mental deficits but leave patients better off than "able-bodied" folks. The person who has a disability today may have a superability tomorrow." ~ Daniel H. Wilson

The summer of 2008, after a year of being on an Apple laptop, my mom's boyfriend, Steve, showed me an app on my laptop called iWeb. iWeb is an app where you can build your own website. I thought it would be fun to make my own website. Before I was introduced to iWeb I always had an idea of building a website all about being the first adaptive snowboarder in the world. I wanted to show other people how I snowboard, and maybe get other people like me to snowboard, too. Now with iWeb, I could. (App stands for "Mobile Application" and is like a software that is used on portable devices such as iPhones and iPads)

I opened up iWeb and started playing around. There was a lot of backgrounds to choose from and I chose my favorite one at the time, then started to build my website. I made all the normal pages you would find on a website's welcome page: about me page, blog page, and a contact page. Then I added photos of me snowboarding and all the photos I had from the Magic of Music and Dance Camp. Then I realized I needed videos on my website to show people how I snowboard and the shows we put on at the

Challenge Aspen's acting camp.

I had never made videos before so I taught myself how to cut up my videos into little videos of the highlights in iMovie so people didn't have to waste their time to see the whole video. After I was done with the videos I put the snowboarding videos on a movie page. Next, I made another page all about the Magic of Music and Dance Camp and added the video of the play we did the year before so I could keep the page up to date.

I realized that I could change the page when we got our copy of the play and cut it up again; keeping it up-to-date every year, and I do. When my website was done I realized the site was becoming more about my hobbies that I love to do rather than all about snowboarding. I was happy about what I had done with it and I published the website on mobileme.com. (me.com is now icloud.com..)

When the website went up it had a long web address and was really hard for my family and friends to get to so I thought it was time to get a real website name. In 2009, after I built up my website and made it more professional, Steve came up to me and asked me if I wanted a better address for my website and I said yes. That night my mom, Steve, and I brain stormed for a perfect name. We thought for a long time on what would go with snowboarding and be easy to remember. Steve came up with Dan

Can Shred. Dan is short for my name, Danielle, and the "Can Shred" is a snowboarding term. So on October 24, 2009 Dan Can Shred was born. (When I tell people I have a website and what the name is, they think that I have a shredding paper business. They don't know the word 'shred' is also a snowboard term to mean ripping it up on the mountain. The next person who asked me if I shred paper up, I should say, "No, but I shred up mountains.")

After Dan Can Shred was born I was hot to trot to build my website. I made my own logo and t-shirt design to have merchandise to sell to people from Café Press. I got the word out by Facebook, Twitter, YouTube, and more. My family helped me with ideas for my website. Also, my best friend, Win, helped me by spreading word of my website and gave me tips and tricks to help me out.

I met Win Charles at the first year of Magic of Music and Dance Camp and we have been best friends ever since. She has CP like me and is also outgoing. She is an amazing artist, snowboarder, and teacher. She has also written her own autobiography to inspire people and tell them what people with CP can really do. She wrote it in honor of her mom who passed away. I read her book and it is amazing. Her book is called "I, Win"; you can buy it on Amazon. (The link is on my website, www.dancanshred.com.) It is a must read. She also is spreading awareness about CP by YouTube and being a triathlete. (Her cousin pulls or pushes her along for the swim, bike, and run.) She is one of the people who inspired me to write this book you are reading right now. I thought if she could write a book, I could, too. We both have a "can do" attitude. We both want to spread CP awareness by working together every day. Check out her art and book on my website and to learn more about Win go to her website http://authorwincharles.com.   I love to share what I am up to by posts on Facebook or Twitter, photos, or making snowboard or highlighting Challenge Aspen's play videos for my friends. Ever wonder if there is a website like Facebook where the info is only about disabilities where you can learn from other people and tell your own story? Well, now you can. The website is called Unique Connect (www.uniqueconnect.org).

My granddad came up with the idea because a lot of people don't know the resources that are right in their own hometown. For example, my family and I didn't know we lived ten minutes away from a hyperbaric chamber. (I will talk about the hyperbaric chamber later in this book.) The website is packed with info from events to stories. My family and I want to keep on growing Unique Connect, so please login to check it out and share your story.

I always love to add new pages to my website and on one of them is a fashion page, because I model for my friend Shelly Wood's store, Watercolors High Fashion.

Here is the story on how I became a model.

In 2009, when I was a sophomore at Park Hill South, I went into Shelly Wood's store to get a dress for homecoming. I heard about her store and had seen the store from the outside but never been in. The first time I walked into the store I was amazed at how many gowns and dresses there were. It was like a girl's dream world. After I picked my dress Shelly asked me if I wanted to be in her next fashion show. I was way excited and said yes!

My first modeling show was in an old building in the downtown of Kansas City that used to be the police station. My mom had to take me early so I could get my hair and makeup done, and learn how to walk down the catwalk. A lot of my friends from high school were there so it was a lot of fun talking backstage. We were on the top level so we could look out the window to see all of the amazing lights of the city. When we practiced walking down the catwalk I had to be escorted by boys because of my balance issues. (And, hey, I didn't mind that, who doesn't want to be escorted by hot boys?) It was fun but hard to know how to walk, where to turn, and when to go. After a while we all had it down and were ready for show time! After that night I had so much fun modeling for Shelly that I wanted to do it again.

Over the years when I have modeled for Shelly I always had fun. She keeps her shows fun, upbeat, and moving. She helps every model with their walk and has them show who they really are. She always says to be yourself, and I always do feel like I'm myself. I love her energy and enthusiasm. Shelly also travels around the United States looking for the "perfect" dresses, accessories, and men's clothing.

She also finds old dresses that need to be worked on. She fixes them up with her style, and they look brand new. If you want to model and be yourself you found the right place. (To look at her dresses go to her website at: www.watercolorshighfashion.com.)

For the past four years when Dan Can Shred came into the world my life had changed a lot. When I am snowboarding, modeling, or helping at an event that show people our disable community and tell them what our world is about, I always show CP awareness without even knowing it. It is like a second nature for me. (I always love and go by Challenge Aspen's quote, "Taking the "Dis" out of Disability.") When I am snowboarding in the winter or acting in the summer I am an ambassador for all of the

Challenge Aspen's kids. (I am also an ambassador for all of the Variety's kids. I will talk about the fun times with them in the next chapter.) When I make people happy it makes me happy too.

When I am working on my website or typing online I always get great comments from my family and friends. One of my friends who follows me on Facebook told me, "I love reading your posts and when I read them you are like a different person." Now that I am thinking of what my friends said and writing this book at the same time I think it is true, because it is hard for me to talk. I think that as you are reading this book it will help you learn more about what CP is and me. I am also learning more about myself as I type this book, which is pretty cool. Some of the disabled people who can't talk use technology to talk with their family and friends. When I type this book on my laptop I propped it up by using a lap desk if I am not at a table. Also I turn on music to help me type faster.

When I am out with friends and they can't understand me I get out my iPhone and open up the notes app or the Proloquo2Go app to talk to them. (Proloquo2Go is an app that is a communication device that is right on your Apple toy, and you don't even need

another big device to carry around. You can buy the app in the App Store.)

Technology is one of our best friends, but not when it is acting up. Some able-bodied people don't have the time to listen to us or think that we can't talk, but when you

hear us you will be amazed.

CHAPTER SEVEN

Everybody has Variety in Them

"A dream doesn't become reality through magic; it takes sweat, determination and hard work." ~ Colin Powell

In the late fall of 2008 my mom and grandparents went to a luncheon to hear a famous woman speak. After the event they ran into a women named Deborah Wiebrecht who is the Director of Variety's Children Charity of Greater Kansas City. (Variety raises money to give wheelchairs, vans, and adaptive bikes to kids with disabilities to help them be mobile and go out with their friends.) Deb told my family all about Variety and then my mom told her about my story and me. After the long talk she invited my mom to bring me to the AMC movie theater to help pass out Christmas gifts to needy kids. (FYI,

I was in school at the time so I didn't meet Deb that day, but I wished I were at that luncheon.)

When my mom picked me up from school she told me the whole story and asked me if I wanted to help out. I said yes right away! (Did I mention that some of the Kansas

City's Chief's football players would be there? Also, I was going to miss a half day of school. How much more awesome can it get?) I was really excited and couldn't wait! The night before I was doing my daily school night routine. I put my Santa hat in my backpack so I wouldn't forget it in the morning. The next morning when mom dropped me off at school at 7:15 AM, I was already counting down until I left at 10:30 AM. It seemed really long, but soon enough, the time had come.

When we got there my mom introduced me to Deb. Deb was outgoing, had so

much energy and still does till this day. I thought Deb was the right kind of person for me. Deb asked me if I could pass out gifts to the kids with the Chiefs players and I said yes. It was a blast to help the Chiefs pass out gifts to the kids and see their smiling faces. After we passed all the gifts out I went over with Deb and the kids and we jammed out to

Christmas songs. I had a blast that day and couldn't wait to help Deb again.

Over the years I helped Deb at many events and became the Young Variety Spokesperson. Being the Young Variety Spokesperson is fun because the kids look up to you. Every time I help Deb I have a lot of fun being with the kids and talking to them. When I make a kid happy it make me happy, too. One year I helped at a one-day baseball camp for disabled kids. I have a lot of fun throwing the ball and encouraging them to hit the ball with the bat. Also, I got to show them the right way to hit the ball with the bat. I felt I was a big sister to the kids. At the end of the day the kids and I got a chance to hit the baseball that was pitched by a KC Royals' baseball player, which was awesome.

We all made a line behind home plate. As I was waiting in line I told Deb how I became a one-hand baseball hitter. When I was in 6th grade we were playing baseball in gym class. When it was my time to bat, my helper, Miss Pam, hit for me and I ran in my walker. It was fun while it lasted and then one day she showed me how to hit the ball with the bat with one hand while I was in my walker. It was hard at first and

I missed balls a lot. I practiced for many days and soon enough I was hitting balls without the tee. I had a blast hitting balls with Miss Pam and my classmates. (Now back to Deb.) At that time I was walking with a cane and I was a little nervous that I might fall because I didn't have my walker, but I was determined to hit the ball.

When it was my turn to bat I walked up to home plate and put my cane into my left hand, got my cane and feet grounded before the person who was handing the bats out gave me a bat. At first, she handed me a plastic bat, and then I said, "No, I want the metal bat." (I meant business, and I wanted to make a good hit.) She gave me the metal bat, and I swung it around before I put the bat up on my right shoulder. I put my game face on and looked at the Royals' baseball player. When we met eye to eye, I knew that he knew that I meant business.

I watched him as he pitched the ball. As the ball got closer to me I swung out with all my might with the bat and hit the ball. I stood there in awe because I hit the ball on the first try. Also, I didn't fall and I hadn't done a one handed hit in a long time. Everybody was yelling for me to run! I dropped the bat, grabbed the cane with my right hand, tucked it under my arm, and took off to first base. When I got there I put my cane down to help me stop and stand up. I was really happy with what I just did. As the other kids hit the ball I ran from base to base until I ran across home plate. At the end of that day I felt really proud that I helped the kids play ball.

Over the years the Royals have teamed up with Variety to raise money. One year in August, the Royals chose Variety for their yearly 5K to help them raise money. In December, before the 5K, I got my own Variety adaptive bike for Christmas. The day that I got it I rode it around in my driveway. I love being on it, I felt I was free and I was going fast like I was on my snowboard again.

When spring came around I got to ride my bike to the park and back to the house.

The park has a big walking path that loops around the whole park. It's made up of two miles and to add two more miles on from the house to the park and back again that would be four miles. I was doing that every day to get ready for the 5K. I got so good riding my bike that I left my mom in the dust and she had to find me at the end of our run. My rule is if you can't keep up, you get left behind.

In late June, we got so much rain that the Missouri River overflowed and flooded the park again. I had to ride my bike in my driveway and work out on the Stairmaster for the rest of the summer. The day before the 5K I felt ready to go and I was so excited to ride my bike in the 5K! The next morning I had to get out of bed at 5:00 AM to get to the

Royals' stadium on time, which was not fun.

When my family and I got there I was wide-awake because I was so excited. There were tons of people walking around, singing, plus a DJ from the Disney Radio. (I am a Disney freak.) I lined up for the 5K with all of the Varity kids on the sidelines so the runners could go first. While I was waiting, my mom was beside me and said, "I want to you to stay with me." I said ok. After a singer sang the national anthem, the starting gun went off and all of the runners took off. Everybody on the sidelines was yelling for them. When the last runner ran past us, the kids started to go, but my mom, Steve, his son, and I waited for my rest of my family to walk by so we could join them.

When we saw them we joined them. The race path was to go around both the

Royals' and the Chiefs' stadiums and then end up crossing home plate in the Royals' stadium. Two minutes into the race I could feel my whole body say to me, "I want to go faster and not go slow." So I put my feet to the pedals and took off. My family saw me and I could hear my mom yelling, "Danielle, come back!" But I was already weaving through people. My stepdad, Steve, and my Aunt Rebecca came running up behind me to run with me. As we were going I was peddling my hardest and looking around all the time so I didn't hit anybody.

Everything was going fine until I passed the first water station. I saw the road went down a little bit and then went up a big hill. (Now going up hills is my biggest challenge. Every time my mom and I get done with our runs at the park she always has to push me up two hills to get to the house.) When I was about to go downhill I slowed down and didn't stop because I didn't want to lose my momentum. I was a little scared I wasn't going to make it up the hill, but Steve talked me into believing in myself.

After Steve's talk, I believed I could make it up the hill. I put my feet to the pedals again to pick up enough momentum so I could make it to the top. I was huffing and puffing. I could hear Steve and Rebecca cheering me on. Hearing them really helped me and I made it up the hill! I was so happy because I made it up the biggest hill by myself for the first time.

The rest of the race was all downhill, which I liked. As the race went on, I was getting tired and I made three turns that were too sharp and I tipped over and fell. I had only my hair band on with no helmet on. I was cringing but wanted to finish the race. Steve and Rebecca helped me back up every time and we kept going. Before we went into the Royals' stadium, Steve told me to smile because I was going to be on the big screen and I was representing all of the Variety kids.

I was still cringing, but I was thinking of what Steve said and he was right. When we got into the stadium, I put on the biggest smile I could and acted like nothing had happened. When I crossed the finish line I felt really happy I did my first 5K, even if my head was hurting. I went on the sideline and was cheering for everybody when they finished the 5K. I will never forget that day. Even though you are hurting inside when you are around people who look up to you, you have to show them that you are okay.

When you are around Deb you never know what will happen. You may think you are at a football game to watch it and the next thing you know you are on the football field playing a game and giving a bike to a Variety kid. Deb has surprised me a lot of times and I want to tell you a story that I will never forget.

In early 2011 my mom told me that Deb had an idea of putting on a Variety Show to raise money for kids with disabilities. Deb asked me to help with the kids in the show, and I said yes. That summer I met the Spinning Tree guys, Andrew and Michael. I started helping them get acts together. It was really fun working with them. I thought I was going to be an assistant director and help the kids do an act just like I do at the Magic of Music and Dance Camp, but that wasn't the case.

In the fall, Deb asked me to help at Ability Day, and I was happy to do so. While I was helping out, Deb told me she had big news to tell me after I did my work. I really wanted to know right then, but Deb said no. I was so anxious to know that I was acting like a little kid before opening a present on Christmas Day. After we were done working we got lunch and went back to the staff room to eat.

Deb finally told me the big news. She told me she showed one of my singing videos to her friend, Drew Six, a country singer. She also said he wanted to sing with me, and I was shocked; I said yes. Then Deb said Drew wanted to write an original song about how the Variety kids feel inside, and the kids and I could email Drew ideas for the song. I was blown away and said yes to emailing him. That night, I thought really long and hard and wrote a list of how I feel as a disability woman, then sent it off to Drew.

I felt really excited that I would be a part of the making of a song. Deb, Drew, and

I were emailing back and forth with the kids and my ideas. I finally met Drew in November at a holiday party. I was happy to meet him and honored to be working with him. Deb took a picture of us for the voting page on the Variety website where people could vote for their favorite Kansas City Star.

Variety was putting on a contest between the stars that was in the show. The star who wins gets named Entertainer of the Year and be on billboards all over Kansas City. I thought that would be so cool to be on a billboard with Drew. Drew and I started to post

'vote for us' everywhere on Facebook and Twitter. I also asked my friends to vote and get the word around school.

There was a patron's party before the show where people who donated the most money were recognized and the acts were announced, as well. Deb wanted Drew and me to sing the song, "We Choose Livin'", so the people would hear it before the show so they could sing along at the show. Drew and I both said yes before the song was even done.

It was hard for Drew to write the song because he didn't know how the disabled kids felt, but with my wisdom and videos on YouTube he learned more about me. In my emails I said that we don't give up and we keep trying. Soon we had a song together and when I heard the song I started to cry because it said what the disabled really feel. We met up to rehearse. It was fun to sing with Drew. Here is my favorite part of the song:

We are the dreamers

We were born to fly

Reachin' for the sky

We love to prove them wrong each and every time We're gonna hold our ground

When reality pushes down

And while they're all busy quittin'

We choose livin'

The night of the patron's party I had a blast singing with Drew, and my new friend Olivia was in front of us videoing us with Drew's camera. At the end of the night,

Young Variety's president, Mark Moberly, announced who won the Entertainer of the Year. When I heard Drew's and my names, I was shocked and excited for Drew because he really earned it for his hard work writing the song. For myself I was happy to be on the billboard with Drew, helping and recognizing the Variety kids. On the night of the show, when I was singing with Drew Six on the Midland stage, I felt really proud of myself because I was using my singing talent to tell people who don't know what disability kids feel inside, while having fun with Drew.

At the end of our song I could hear everyone yelling and clapping. When I heard that sound I felt even happier. When the curtain went down I got to stay on stage to sing "Defying Gravity" from Wicked with all of the kids and Tina Maddigan who was the lead in "Mamma Mia" on Broadway! I had the best night singing and hanging out

backstage with new and old friends. It was a night I will never forget.

In 2012 we got the song, "We Choose Livin'", on iTunes and all of the money will go to Variety. You should buy the song to support Variety; it is an amazing song to hear. Every time I am with Deb and helping Variety I feel really happy I can help kids like me. I love making them happy and showing them you can do anything if you put your mind to it. If you have an organization by you that needs help with disabled kids you should go out and help. It will make you happier if you do.

http://www.VarietyKc.org

CHAPTER EIGHT

Life in College with CP

"If you're trying to achieve, there will be roadblocks. I've had them; everybody has had them. But obstacles don't have to stop you. If you run into a wall, don't turn around and give up. Figure out how to climb it, go through it, or work around it." ~ Michael Jordan

When I was a senior in high school I had a lot of decisions to make on what I wanted to do in my life. Whether or not I wanted to go to college, and if so, where. My family is really supportive of me and wants to help me in life. I wanted to go to school to do more acting which I love to do. My mom took me to Park University that is five minutes from my house to look around.

It was on a big hill so I would have my exercise everyday if I decided to go there. The campus was the most beautiful place I had ever seen. I passed it every day to go to high school and been there when I was young, but never took in the beauty of it until now. One of the buildings looks like Hogwort's Castle or Cinderella's Castle, which was awesome. We took a tour of the whole campus and part of the school is underground. It was really cool to be underground but my iPhone won't work down there. (When iMessage came out I was really happy because I could finely text my family if I needed to. See, iMessage is an apple technology that allows you to message other iphones when you were near a wireless signal.)

After the tour we went to see what they had for majors. You may know me by now; I went straight to the acting table. When I got to the table I met the two acting teachers, Andrea Southard and Janie Peak. I know Janie because I acted with her son, Will, in high school. They were really nice. They showed me what their acting department did, and I really liked it. There was only one down side to this department, it is only a minor. I had to keep that in mind. After we talked with Andrea and Janie we ran into a teacher name Walter Kisthardt who is the director of the social work program. We talked for a while and I told him what I did at Magic of Music and Dance Camp. He told me that I could help kids in music therapy. I really liked that idea and maybe I would like to do that. At the end of that fun day I had a lot of think about.

In March, when I was in Snowmass for my spring break I wanted to go check out

Colorado Mountain College (CMC) because I wanted to be near my friends and be where I love to be. My mom and I went to the campus in Aspen and took a tour with a staff member. I really liked the place and the small classrooms. At the end of the tour I asked if there were any acting classes there.

She told me that they didn't have any acting classes there, but the CMC campus in Spring Valley did. So Mom, Steve, and I went to that campus to look around. There was no one there so we couldn't take the whole tour. We could only go into the main building and walk around outside. I really liked the landscape but I wished there was someone there so I could look at everything. At the end of our trip to CMC I realized it would be hard to go to CMC with my family still living in Parkville, because I couldn't call them up and ask them to come by if I needed help. So I thought Park U would be my best choice.

When I got back to school I had to get ready to take the ACT Test to get into Park U. My mom and I went to the bookstore to get an ACT book to get ready for the test.

Every night after I did my homework my mom helped me get ready for the test. It was really hard work but it was worth it. My Language Arts teacher who gave me the ACT Test also made special arrangements for me to take it so I would have more time. I got out of three of my classes for four days so I could take my time and not rush through it. I know I used 15 hours in my life to take the ACT Test and many more to get ready for it.

It was really hard work but at the end of it I was really happy that I took the test.

When my ACT scores came in my high school sent my scores to Park U. A couple of weeks later I got a letter from Park U. I opened it up and read it right away. When I saw that I got in I got way excited; I was jumping up and down in my seat. Later that summer, Deborah McAuthor, the Director of Special Services, asked me to do a math and spelling tests to see which classes I needed to take. (Spelling and math were low on my ACT Test.) I didn't want to take the tests because I already did the ACT Test, but I put my big girl pants on and did them.

During the whole summer my family helped me get ready for college life. My

Granddad called his friend, James Landrum, who is the Executive Director of Truman Neurological Center (TNC) Community, to see if he could help. TNC helps take care of people with disabilities that live in group homes around the Kansas City area. James asked his friends, Ann Johnson and Mary Beth Johnson, to help on this project, too. (The project was called Danielle's Project.) We had a ton of meetings to get me ready to go to Park U. We looked for the right tools to help me talk to people, a reading app to help me read my textbooks, and all the stuff I needed to live in the dorm.

My mom asked me a lot of times if I wanted to live at home with her or in the dorms at school. I told her that I wanted the whole college experience. She said okay but she was scared for me. I told her I would be okay. At the end of the summer we had an interview with two women who worked at TNC to see which one would be best to help me at school. It was fun to meet them both but one was really up beat, positive, and bubbly. She was just like me; so I picked her. Her name is Amanda Weatherby.

I was so excited to start my first year of college! Two weeks before classes started I went to get my college ID. My ID was my key to get into my dorm, the gym, my library card, and my credit card to eat in the café. (Four ways to use my ID and it is all in one card, how awesome is that!) After I got my ID my friend, Jody, wanted me to try to get into my dorm. I had been to the dorms to check out some of the rooms, and they were awesome! When you walk into one you will see the living room in front of you, to your right is a little kitchenette, and when you go right or left you will see a bathroom and a bedroom with two beds in it. It was pretty awesome.

When I got to the dorms, Jody showed me to my dorm. I had to put my ID up to a box that read it and unlocks the door so I could get into the building. The doors were so heavy for me to get open, but there was a handicapped button that I could push to make the doors open by themselves. My dorm was on the first floor so I could get out of the building if there was a fire. (FYI: One time we had a fire drill at 2:00 AM, which was no fun.)

We walked down a long hallway to get to my new home for the next ten months: Room 103. To open my door I had to do the same thing that I did outside, but I had to push the door open by myself because there was no handicap button. Once I got into the dorm I turned to my right automatically because the lights were on and I could see bright colors everywhere. When I went into my room my eyes almost popped out of my head because my room was decorated in bright colors like in the hippy era.

It was like my dream bedroom come true, but I didn't know about this or help plan it out. I was so excited about my new room that I didn't want to go back home. Everybody was there that helped with the Danielle's Project that helped to finish my room. I loved everything and thanked everyone for helping me make going to college possible.

Kerri Schaefer, who helps run the dorms, allowed me to move in the day before everybody moves into the dorms, before all the craziness happens. So my mom and Amanda helped me move in. It took all day, but by 5:00pm we were all done. My mom asked me if I wanted to spend the night at the house or at the dorm all by myself. I told her that I wanted to stay at the dorm.

She was scared for me but I told her that I would be fine. When I am by myself, I love it because I can turn up my music and jam out. No one can yell at me to turn it down. She said okay and I was happy and great all night long. (FYI: I forgot to tell you that I asked Kerri if I could have no roommates; only suite mates, and she said yes. When you have CP you need to get up really early to get ready to be on time to class. I need a lot of space for myself to get ready for the day. Also, it's really hard for me to be quiet and I don't want to wake anyone up. Today I am better on being quiet.)

The next day was move-in day for everybody. I got up early to get ready for the day because I didn't want to meet my suitemates in my PJs. When the first one came in, I introduced myself and asked if she needed help moving in. She said no she don't need help because her mom was there to help. Over the whole year I tried to fit in and hang out with my suitemates but they were always gone and went home on the weekends. The next year I got two new suitemates whose names were Sally and Anna and I got to hang out with them more, which was awesome.

Life in the dorms was a lot of fun. Our Residential Assistant (RA) for our floor put on a lot of parties so everyone on our floor could hang out together. (RA is a person who is in charge of their dorm floor and makes sure that everything is running smoothly.) We even had dance parties in the hallway late at night, which was a blast! When you live on campus you can go to a lot of activities with your friends like Bingo, Park Idol, and even go on a ghost hunt. I went to the activities when I didn't have a lot of homework to do. When I went to them I had a lot of fun and I got to hang out with friends and make new ones, too.

When it comes to schoolwork I am a hard worker. Here is what a normal day at school is like for me. In the morning I get up really early to get ready and eat before Amanda gets to the dorm. For breakfast I eat yogurt or drink a shake that Amanda has made the night before. Amanda has her own ID to get in, but if she forgets it she will text me and I have to run down the hall to let her in.

If we are all ready to go before we have to go to class, we just hang out and talk, or she would help me with homework if I had it. When it was time to go, Amanda put on my backpack on and we would set off for class. Amanda would carry my backpack because if I would have a heavy backpack on I would lose my balance and I would fall.

And we wouldn't want that now, would we? Also, she walks with me to make sure that I won't fall.

When we are in the classroom we set down side-by-side and Amanda takes notes while I listen. She takes notes for me because I write too slowly. When she can't come I try to take notes but I am slow and miss a lot of important stuff. So now when she is not there, I ask my neighbor to take notes for me. When I have an in-class assignment to do Amanda and I whisper back and forth to get the assignment done. After class, if we have free time between classes we do homework or hang out at "The Smart Market" with our friends.

At lunch, Amanda helps me carry my plate of food to the table so I won't drop it. (At nighttime the people who work at the café help me out. Also, when the weather is really bad the campus security drives me down to the dorm. I am really happy about that.)

After the school day is done, we go back to the dorm to do homework. We do as much as we can together before Amanda has to go pick up her kids. When she leaves I do as much homework as I can that night. It is hard to do homework by yourself when you have a challenge. If an able-bodied person has a page of 25 math problems to do and it takes them one hour to do, it would take me like four hours to do by myself. If I were going to college by myself with no helper it would take me like ten years to complete. I am happy to have Amanda to help me out and hang out with as a friend.

When I have a reading assignment to do in one of my textbooks, I have my laptop read it to me. I get all my textbooks on PDF so I can copy the chapter that I need to read in an app that is called Kurzweil 300 and have it read it to me. I am really happy that I have that app. If I didn't have that app I would be reading one chapter all night long and couldn't get other things that need to be done. Speaking of reading, let's talk about writing. It takes me a long time to write a paper on a topic that the teacher gives you. So Amanda and I work together and get the paper done. After the paper is done I take it to the Academic Support Center (ASC) to have it proof read. The ASC is where students go and get help on their assignments.

I hate writing papers for school. When I was in my second year of college I was in an acting class where I had to write a ten-minute play that was based off a real life experience that happened in my life. I had thought about it for a long time and thought I could write about how I became the first adaptive snowboarder in the world. Remember how I became the first adaptive snowboarder back in Chapter Three?

Well, I had the video game in there and I set the timing for Christmas Day. I made all of my characters with my Challenge Aspen friends' names to make up my family in the play. I added two brothers in it to have brother and sister fights to make it funnier. (Hey, I might have been an only child, but I have been in the middle of a lot of them at my friend's house and trust me, they got wild and crazy.) I named myself Zoey because it was my favorite character to play in SSX Tricky.

As I type this play I realize I love to type freely and not have others tell me what to type. Also, I love it because people can hear my real voice. At that time Win's book "I, Win" just came out and over the years I have a lot of my friends encouraging me to write this book. I guess it takes a BFF and myself to write a book and a play to make me write this book. The right timing is everything.

The worst time of college for me is a night before a test. When Amanda leaves I would have my head in the books until my brain says, "It's time for you to go to bed." I

give all my 100% hard work to get ready for a test. Trust me I don't like doing tests, but I need to. (FYI if there were no tests in college I would love it.) The next day when it was time to take my test I didn't go to class. Instead, Amanda and I went to Deborah McAuthor's office to get my test, and then go to a free room so I could take the test. We have go into another room so Amanda could read the test to me and I could tell her my answers so we wouldn't bother anyone who was taking the same test. Every time before a test I get so nervous, but when I get in the room to start the test I get really happy when I know a lot of the answers right away. After I take a test I feel happy and relieved that the test is out of the way and I knew that I passed it.

I know sometimes people get stuck with a teacher they don't like at all and they have to deal with them all semester long. Well, I got a teacher that didn't go by the disability rules. Here is the story. (FYI, I forgot her name because Amanda and I didn't want to say her name.) It was the first day of new classes and a new school year. I was excited to meet all of my new teachers, but I didn't know that one of my teachers didn't go by the disability rules.

On the first day we went to class early to pick the best seat so I could learn really well. I chose to be in the first row so I could see everything; which was the biggest mistake of my life, now that I am looking back on it. When the teacher walked in she introduced herself and then did roll call to see if everybody was there who was in the class. She did it row by row, but when she got to Amanda and me she said, "I am not calling your name because you are not on my list," to Amanda.

She said it out loud so everybody could hear it. She did it every day and then Amanda and I got the first clue on what she was like.

One day after class we went into her office and to tell her it wasn't necessary to call on Amanda every day. Everybody in the class knows that I need an assistant because of my disability. She says that she wants me to be like everybody else and not have special treatment. As time went on she got harder on me and changed my whole system that Amanda and I have been working on for a year that my whole family set up before I went to Park U.

The teacher wanted me to write papers and do tests on my own, because she believes that I was cheating with help, but I wasn't. I was doing the same work as everybody else, but in a different way. Hello, when you have a disability and when you need help you get it because you can't do it all by yourself.

When I was writing her papers it took me all my night typing by myself. I did a

14 pages paper all by myself with a little help from Amanda. I didn't like the long nights of typing but when the paper was done I was proud at myself. With testing that was a whole different ball game. On testing day I had to pack up my laptop and headphones to go to Deborah McAuthor's office by myself to take the test.

When I got to Deborah McAuthor's office, she helped get me set up in one of the desk cubbies in the library right by her office door. She put a flash drive into my laptop which had the test on it. I opened the test up and copied the whole test and pasted it into my Kurzweil 3000 app so it would read it to me. It wasn't that bad when it was all multiple and matching questions, but with essay questions that is another story. When a test is all multiple and matching questions it takes me a little over an hour to take the test, but when there are essay questions involved it takes me like two hours. When the tests are longer like midterms and finals, it take me five to ten hours to complete a test. At that time I didn't realized why it took me so long to complete a test on my own and why I was faster with Amanda. Now, as I type this, I think I go faster with Amanda because I think when I talk out loud to someone that I am comfortable with, I can think faster and he or she can write down what I say. Those testing days felt like I was in a black hole that I couldn't get out of because I was testing underground with no sunlight.

During the whole semester when I had to go to that teacher's class, Amanda and I were dragging our feet because we didn't want to go to class, but I had to. Also, it was hard for us to act like nothing was going on and pretend to be happy in the classroom, but we had to.

One day after class Amanda did a brave thing for me. After everybody was out of the classroom, even me, she went back in and told the teacher how the disability rules works. After that everything went downhill from there, but I was really happy that Amanda did that for me. I worked so hard in that class, but in the end I got a C. I hope that no one will get a teacher like the one I had.

At the end of my second year of college Amanda and I realized that social work wasn't for me because you have to do a lot of paperwork and talk to a lot of people. It would be hard for me because I type really slowly and it is hard to talk to people because of my speech. Amanda and I looked in the school handbook of majors. We found that they had a graphic design major. We both thought it would be perfect for me because I love to work on my website and make videos. So I signed up for classes to be all ready to go next year.

That summer, when I was in Snowmass, I was running around with my musical friends to sing and act. At the end of the summer I realized that what I really wanted to do was go to school for acting. I went online and looked at the acting programs at Colorado Mountain College (CMC). I learned you have to work in the stage area a lot and you get to write plays. I thought this would be perfect for me. It is funny how you have to make a big loop to found out where you really need to be is right in your heart. When you know

what you really want to do with your life, do it, and don't let other people tell you what to do. I hope that TNC will work more on the Danielle Project to help more people like me go to college to follow their dreams on what they truly want to do in their life.

CHAPTER NINE

Movement is Good Medicine for CP

"Life is like riding a bicycle. To keep your balance, you must keep moving." ~ Albert Einstein

When people have CP their muscles are always on and get tighter and tighter as we age. Every day we stretch or workout to keep our mobility, stay strong, and be healthy. Over the years I have done yoga, Pilates, horseback riding, gymnastics, the Stairmaster, and had a personnel trainer. All of these things helped me a lot while I was growing up. In 2011 my family and I found a Hyperbaric Healing Institute that was ten minutes away from my Parkville house. The Hyperbaric Chamber has helped me in a lot of amazing ways and I would love to share my journey with you.

In late fall of 2011, my family and I went to the Hyperbaric Healing Institute to try and see if the Hyperbaric Chamber would be good for me. The Hyperbaric Chamber is a big chamber that people go into to get oxygen to help heal from an injury, a stroke, CP, and a lot more. The owners, Lisa and David Deister, have a daughter named Tatum, who also has CP. They researched for a long time to find something that would help Tatum to move better and they found a Hyperbaric Chamber in Arizona.

They went down there for many summers and did the treatment. It really helped

Tatum and they realized they didn't want to stay in Arizona for a whole month anymore, so they started their own Hyperbaric Healing

Institute (HHI) right in the Kansas City area. (They had to stay in Arizona for a month because Tatum had to go into the

Hyperbaric Chamber 40 times for CP.) For CP you have to be in the chamber for an hour and a half and when you get out you have to wait three hours to get back in. You can get in the chamber two times a day, five days a week.

If you do more you will get way too tired because of the increase of oxygen that you are getting. The Federal Drug Administration considers 100% oxygen is a drug so I went to a doctor who was familiar with hyperbaric therapy and received a prescription. The prescription details how much oxygen to be given and length of time to stay in the chamber. It is a lot like taking a dive under water.

Before I went to the HHI, Lisa and David emailed a list to my family of what to wear and not to wear when you are in the chamber. You can only wear cotton clothes. What not to wear are: makeup, hair product, partum, cologne, lotions, and jewelry. (If you wear all the stuff that I listed and wear clothes that are not cotton, you will blow up in flames, and we don't want that.) So I mostly wear my PJs because in the email, they also said, it will get cold when you get into the chamber. On the day that my family and I went to the HHI I was really excited and couldn't wait to see what my outcome would be when I got out of the chamber for my first time.

When we got there David had to measure everybody's necks who were going into the chamber with me. He did this because we had to wear hoods to keep our own oxygen to ourselves; if we get too much oxygen in the chamber, flames will start to appear. After he got everybody's neck measurements, he went to cut holes in the rings we had to wear around our necks so our hoods could stay on. When he came back with our rings we had to help each other to put them on. The material in the middle of the ring is latex. Latex is a type of plastic. We had to help each other out by stretching it out to get it over our heads so we wouldn't rip our hair out of our heads. (Trust me, I got a lot of hairs ripped out over the years, and sometimes an earring or two, and that hurt.)

Before we got into the chamber, Lisa showed us how to work the dials to get our oxygen, how to put the hoods on, and she also told us to pop our ears on the way down.

When you are in the chamber it feel like you are deep sea driving, but you are not. When I got into the chamber I was amazed at how big it was. It could hold eight people at once and there was a TV in there so we could watch a movie or a TV show.

One summer day I was in the chamber with kids and their moms and dads there to help them; all together it was 10 or 11 people in there at once, just like a clown car. When we were in there, for the whole time we talked to each other, but it was hard because we had to yell over the air that was blowing.

When we were done, Lisa helped me walk out. As I was walking I was really wobbly and Lisa told me that was a good sign that the chamber was a good thing for me to do. So after that day I did three rounds of hyperbaric treatments. My first round I did 50 dives and the last two I did 40. So that would add up to be 130 treatments, wow! (FYI; between each round you have to wait for three months to do it again. If you don't you wouldn't see any outcomes.)

In my three hours off between hyperbaric treatments I didn't lay low, I moved over to the other side of the HHI to do intensive PT with Tiffany or Kate. They are awesome to work with! One the first day of

PT, I had to get evaluated to see what I could do and see what I needed to work on. First I laid down on a red table so Tiffany could stretch me out and take measurements of my body to see how flexible I was. After I did some tests on the table she wanted to see how I walked up and down the stairs. I don't know how many times I walked up and down the stairs, but it was a lot. Then I had to stand up from a chair and get up from the floor without a wall all by myself. Getting up from the chair was really hard; I could do it, but not very well. Now, getting up from the floor was impossible to do.

Every time I put a leg up and tried to push off of it, I fell over like a rolly-polly bug. (FYI: she videotaped everything so my family and I could see it.) When my first round of PT was done she gave me a CD of all of the videos and I put them in one video and put it on YouTube so my friends could see. You can also watch the video on my website at www.dancanshred.com. Over time I got better getting up from a chair and even got up from the floor with both of my legs pushing off and standing up without a step.

After the first day of PT, I started walking on the treadmill and playing games that helped my balance while I was wearing a suit called a thera suit. A thera suit trains your muscles to be in the right place and work in the right way. When astronauts come back to Earth they put the same suits on to retain their muscles and get their land legs back. The suit was made up of a vest, shorts, kneepads, shoes, and in between were a lot of bungees. When Tiffany put it on me she helped me walk around until I got used to it. It felt really weird at first, as if I had a straitjacket on.

Tiffany told me if I fell down when I was in the suit she would have to pick me up, because nobody could stand up by themselves when they are in the suit. So, I tried my hardest not to fall, but one day, one of the hooks on a bungee cord behind one of my knees magically decided to hook on my other kneepad and made me fall down hard. This didn't happen one time, it happened four or five times on the same day. That hook would get some whoopings back from me.

When I am on the treadmill or doing footwork, I am in a cage, bungeed to the cage, so I can stay in one spot. If I go too far either way, I get bounced back to the middle, just like a marionette. It was hard to get used to it and do my work at the same time, but I did it. I did a ton of stuff from kicking bowling pins down, throwing stuffed animals into a basketball hoop, and a lot more.

I even got to throw and catch a ball while I was standing up all by myself without leaning against a wall or anything! Even though I was 19 and playing an old fashioned kids game of ball, I felt the joy of being a kid again, because I had never felt this of joy. When I was on the playground in elementary school I was always in my walker and never had the chance to play ball.

I even asked my dad to join in the fun so he could see what I could do and I wanted to play ball with him just like an able-bodied kid. It was a blast! Later, I was able to throw a ball while I was kneeling down on one knee. It was really hard at first, but it got easier and easier every day.

While I was doing my work at the HHI, I gained a lot more freedom and could do more stuff on my own. For example, one day when I went home I tried to dance. After a while I turned on the song "Cha Cha Slide", and when I heard the first "jump", I jumped!

That was the first time I had ever jumped in my whole life! I laughed so hard I fell down. I felt my joy blasting out of me because I was dancing really well without my walker! I always wanted to dance without my walker. I had danced a lot of Irish jigs when I was at an Elders concert, but that was the only dance that I could do really well without my walker before I got introduce to the HHI. Now that I have done my hard work in PT, I

feel freer to dance how I want to without my walker and with fewer falls. Here is an example of this in a story.

Last summer, on July 4th, 2013, I was in the Old Fashioned 4th of July Parade with my Challenge Aspen friends. Every year we help build the float for the parade and we theme it around the play we are going to put on at the Magic of Music and Dance Camp that year. We tell people about it so they can come see our play. That year we were going to do "The Sound of Music", one of the loveliest musicals of all time. A lot of my friends were there to be in the parade. Mack and Rachel, who are the new head directors of the camp, were there, too, which was really fun. Before the parade, when we were getting everything ready to go, Mack came up to me to talk and catch up from the last time we saw each other.

Everything was going great until he asked me, "Are you ready for your big dance number?" All I could do was drop my jaw and nod my head up and down. I was in shock. I couldn't even speak and asked what number I would be doing. He didn't have time to tell me because it was time to load everyone onto the float. I had fun singing with everybody and pretended to play the guitar in the parade, but in the back of my mind all I was thinking about was what song I was going to dance to. I was so nervous.

After the parade, Mack finely told me what the song was that I would be dancing to - "Sixteen, Going on Seventeen." I was excited, nervous, and scared all at the same time. I was so happy to dance in the play for my first time at the camp, but what if I fall and make a fool of myself? But I was happy to have a guy to help hold me up. Who would play my dancing partner, Rolf? I hoped he would be really strong.

At the first day of camp I was excited and nervous to see who I would be singing and dancing with. When I knew that I was going to sing and dance with my friend Chad I was really happy because he is tall and looks strong. As the week went on Rachel and Nicole, the new pianist, helped with our song and dance.

The plan was that Chad would sing, we would dance, I would sing, and then we do a big hug at the end. First we sang the whole song once without dancing. (FYI: Rachel and Nicole cut the first part of the song out, but Chad and I knew the whole song and wanted to sing it all and we did.) After we sang the song, we worked on the dance. All four of us came up with a dance that Chad and I could manage. The dance went like this:

We spun one-way and then the other way, and then I did a twirl under Chad's arm. It was hard at first and I got my wrist yanked a few times, but as the week went on it got easier and easier.

On Thursday, when we run through the play twice, we had a few mess ups, but we had it down by the end of the day. The next day was the big day, show day. I was so nervous that something would go wrong, but I was happy because I knew we had one more run through with lights and mikes before the real show. Everybody got to the theater on time but we were running behind for the first time in 16 years.

All we could do was see where everybody's place in each scene was, without singing. When I got off the stage after we did the placing for the Von Trapp kids line up,

I was horrified and scared that I didn't get to run through Chads and my part. I was 100times more scared that I would lose my balance and fall because we didn't practice. I knew if I thought that way I was going to do what I was thinking. All that I could do was to stay calm and hope for the best.

As the play was about the begin I ran to my place in the wings where I was going to stay doing the whole show and help with the background singing of the song "The

Sound of Music." I was having a fun time singing backstage and watching all of my friends singing and acting before it was time for me to go on. When the lights came up on my scene I had butterflies in my stomach and I didn't have my microphone headset on yet and I was supposed to go on in two minutes.

Luckily, I saw Crystal right beside me with my microphone, but she was looking the other way trying to find me. I tapped on her back and she turned around and helped me and my buddy put my microphone on. As we were almost to the time where the kids had to march in, we had a little trouble getting the box clipped to my skirt, but we got it on just in the nick of time. When I was out on stage my butterflies went away but they came back when Chad walked in and my buddy let go of me, so I was only with Chad. I could feel my whole body tense up, because this was my first time singing and dancing with my friend without my walker.

When he was singing to me I could feel my body leaning in to him and knew that

I would have to pull my body up so I wouldn't fall into him. It was hard to pull myself up, but I did it. When it was time to dance, all the tension in my body went away, because I was moving and having fun with Chad. As we went on with our act I felt really good.

At the end when we hugged, I felt happy and relieved that we pulled off that act together. When the lights went down, I went back to my seat with the biggest smile on my face because I knew that we did it! Who knows what the future will hold?

I want to give you one more example of how the Hyperbaric Healing Institute helped me in being healthy. When I was at Park U I was taking a health class. In the class I had to do a health project for 16 weeks. The project was intended to show you how healthy you are. The first part of the project is to test all parts of your body, like strength, flexibility, and how fast you walk or run 1.5 miles. After you have done all of the tests, you plan out your daily workout and then, after the 16 weeks are up, you have to do all of the tests again to see how you do.

One of the tests was to see how fast you walk or run 1.5 miles. I asked my teacher how I could do this because of my CP. She said that I could cut down the miles and do it however I wanted to. You maybe know me by now; I didn't want to cut done the miles. When I went home for Labor Day weekend I asked my mom if she would help me with my tests, and she said yes. I did all tests that I could do at home; all that was left was the walk or run for 1.5 miles test. We went to my high school's track. My mom asked me if I wanted my walker and I said no, because I wanted to see how I would do after my two rounds of hyperbaric treatments.

On the way to the track I did math in my head to see how many laps around the track I needed to do to walk or run 1.5 miles. I remembered when I was in high school the P.E. teachers said one mile is four laps around the track. Four laps around is a mile then add a half of a mile is two laps, so I would have to do six laps in all. Now that is a lot! When we got there I picked a line on the track to start my test. My mom got out her phone so she could time me. (FYI: she had flip-flops on and she had our dog, Jewels, too. I had tennis shoes on and nothing in my hands. So who got left behind in dust? You got it, my mom.)

When my mom started the timer I started a steady jog. I jogged as fast and the best as I could. As I got half- way though my six laps I was getting tired. My mom asked me if I wanted to stop. I yelled as best as I could, "I… want to… but I… want to… keep… going!" As I kept going I had a good rhythm with my arms and my whole body. Some times I fell down two or three times and I jumped back up and kept going. When I was coming up to the last lap I asked my mom if I could have a helping hand on my last lap because I was so tired, and she gave me her hand and we ran together on the last lap. All the way she said, "You can do it!" That really helped me. When I ran across my starting line I fell down and my mom stopped the timer. I was so tired that I couldn't even move but I was really proud at myself on what I just did. I asked my mom what my time was and she said 38 minutes and 45 seconds.

The Hyperbaric Healing Institute has helped me move more freely over the years but there is one more step that really helped me after I did a full round of being in the Hyperbaric chamber and doing PT: it was speech therapy. After my first round of Hyperbaric, David suggested that I call his friend, Paul, up to see if he could help me talk better. (FYI: the hyperbaric chamber helped me talk better, also.) David told me that he helped Tatum a lot and thought that he could help me, too.

My family and I called Paul up and made an appointment. (FYI: he doesn't have an office, he comes to you.) At the time I was living in my dorm at Park U so he came there and I let him into my dorm, Room 103. The first time Paul and I met he asked me about my eating, swallowing, and he looked to see how well I could move my tongue around. After he saw what I could do he showed me his little machine.

The machine is a little box with buttons on it, just like a Walkie Talkie, but different. It is called E-Stem therapy. At the top there were two in ports where Paul plugs in two cords, and at the other end of the cord were round things that pop on round pads that stick onto your face. He put them on my face where my muscles needed the most work. (FYI: he put the pads on one side of my face and then he put them on the other side on his next visit and visa versa.)

After the pads were in place, he placed tape over them so they wouldn't move. (My least favorite part was when we would have to rip the tape off at the end.) As he is doing this he tells me what the machine does. It sends electrodes to my face to stimulate my muscles to work in a different way. I was scared at first, but when he turned it on it was okay with no hurting, just a tingling. If Paul put a pad in the wrong spot it hurt so bad and then he had to move it again. It took time to get used to it. It took 30 minutes to do with the machine on for 15 seconds and off for 10 and it cycled like this for the whole 30 minutes, so your face can get a little break. There are different levels that you can go to, like if you can't feel the tingling, or if you are ready to move up a level you can. Over time I went up the levels and my highest level that I got up to was 12 or 13.

Over time my speaking, eating, and my swallowing got better. Even my face got more even, just like a face-lift. (When I had to renew my state photo ID I was amazed how much my face had changed.) My mom saw it, too, so in the summertime my mom got Gran and some of her friends together to have one big face lift party. It was fun and funny for me to see Paul doing the treatment on somebody else and see his or her faces move. Everybody was telling me if I kept doing this treatment I would look young forever, and I think they are right. I am really happy with all of the outcomes that I got from this treatment; Speaking, eating, swallowing, and I don't want to forget about singing, too.

Exercising is important for everybody to keep healthy, strong, and keep us moving. For people with challenges like me we have to do something every day so we can keep moving for the rest of our life. Our muscles are always on and if we don't exercise we are going to get weaker every day. We have to fight every day to keep moving. So if you are lying around the house watching TV or reading this book, I'll say put this book down, do a workout inside or run/play outside and when you are done you can come back and read the last chapter of this book. It would be worth it.

"Remember to get plenty of fresh oxygen and exercise daily" - Danielle

CHAPTER TEN

The Journey Keeps Rolling

"Life is a song - sing it. Life is a game - play it. Life is a challenge - meet it. Life is a dream - realize it. Life is a sacrifice - offer it. Life is love - enjoy it." ~ Sai Baba

Thank you for letting me share my stories and adventures with you. I hope you will follow your own dreams with no one telling you what to do. As I am typing to you right now I am thinking how much fun I had working on this book so you could read my life story, and finally hear my voice.

Years ago my friends and family encouraged me to write a book. Every time I heard, "You should write a book because you are so inspiring." I replied with a no. I said no because I was only thinking of my past. As I was growing up I didn't like to read or write because it was hard for me. (But I loved to make up short stories.) The summer I

was about to go into high school my reading tutor took me to the bookstore so I could pick a book to read.

I spotted the first "Magic Tree House" book and that whole summer I read a book from that series every day because I loved to imagine that I was in the story and in a whole different world. I worked harder on my reading and writing. Now I can read harder books and write this book that you are reading right now, but I still have some challenges.

On the first day of working on this book I wasn't sure I was able to type this whole book by myself. Every day when I was typing away I had fun going down memory lane and when I stopped for a few days because I didn't feel like typing, I thought of my BFF Win working on her next book every day. It made me get back to typing away on this book. It's good to have a BFF because when one of them is down, the other one helps get them back on their feet, and we do that. It takes two to do amazing things. Also, as I type this book I had to learn more about myself. I feel like a different person now than I did from the first day on typing this book. I feel like I can inspire more people around the world to follow their dreams.

I am happy my friends and family pushed me to write this book and believed in me. They also helped me in all the hard and fun times throughout my life. When I wanted to snowboard, act, model, sing, hang glide, or walk on my own, they didn't hold me back. I am happy to have grown up in a family that helped me be the best that I can be. I want to thank my family for pushing me, believing in me, and supporting me in who I am today.

Every day Win, Max, Rochelle, and I, and whoever else who has Cerebral Palsy or another challenge, are fighting to make what we want to do a reality. We don't listen to other people when they put limits on what we can and cannot do. We do want to try to have a Zip-A-Dee-Do-Da day every day.

I hope my book teaches you more of what it is like to have Cerebral Palsy, and inspires you to do what you want to do and follow your own dreams. Nothing is impossible if you believe in yourself. Until next time, see you on the fly side.

Dream it; Live it!

Danielle's Fund for Challenged Girls

My grandparents love to help people and non-profit organizations in the Kansas City area. Together they came up with the Fred H. and Shirley J. Pryor Foundation to give money to people in need. While they were helping me with my daily needs when I was at their house, they realized they wanted to help other girls like me who have any disabilities. They found there were a lot of girls who didn't have any money to do what I do like horseback riding. One day they went to the Women's Foundation of Kansas City and opened a foundation called Danielle's Fund for Challenged Girls. This fund helps girls with challenges do fun stuff like anybody else and have a fun girls night out! I am really thrilled my grandparents came up with this idea so girls like me can do fun stuff and not be home all day. Here is the description from the Women's Foundation pamphlet.

Danielle's Fund for Challenged Girls – Founded December 2000 by Shirley and

Fred Pryor, Sherilyn Coulter, and Rebecca Pryor Phillips. In the spirit of Danielle Pryor Coulter, this fund is intended to help the physically challenged turn their disabilities into possibilities. To make a donation please visit http://www.Wfgkc.org

Learn More about Danielle

This is my story and I live it:

I like to spend time on my computer, hang out with my friends, and play games. My favorite game is solitaire. I enjoy reading books, especially mysteries. I also love to write plays and stories.

Acting is a special interest. I have been acting since I was five years old. My first role was as a pirate in The Messing Room. Every summer I participate in Challenge Aspen Music and Dance Camp. You can read more about Challenge Aspen in Challenge Aspen Plays.

I also do adaptive snowboarding through Challenge Aspen. I was the first adaptive snowboarder. I had been adaptive skiing since I was five. When I was nine years old I decided I would like to snowboard. At that time there was no adaptive snowboard equipment.

My ski instructor, Rich Ganson, and I were given the first experimental version of an adaptive snowboard made by Bobby Palm. It was made of PVC pipe and very simple. We spent a week developing it so that it was fully functional and more adaptive for different needs and sizes. We broke the first one rather quickly catching too much air over a big jump. Tuff equipment for a tuff girl!!! Once we had added the needed changes and parts, it was brought to a great adaptive equipment company called Freedom Factory. They then built a version for all kids and adults with challenges so they could explore snowboarding. This new version was used for the first group of Iraqi war vets that came to Snowmass for rehabilitation and was a huge part of their growth. Some of this can be seen in the documentary "Beyond Iraq" which received accolades at the Sundance film festival.

Danielle Coulter has published the following books and they can be purchased on Amazon.com

If Dan can Shred You Can Too

Zoe and the Great Easter Egg Hunt

Zoe and the Missing Clown Costume

The Hard Life of Zoe

Zoe and the Ghostly Mall

CPSIA information can be obtained
at www.ICGtesting.com
Printed in the USA
LVOW10s2343191217
560343LV00055B/3858/P